Learn about ... TEXAS

FRESHWATER FISHES

A Learning and Activity Book
Color your own field guide to the fishes that swim in Texas' rivers, streams and lakes.

Editorial Direction and Text by
Georg Zappler

Art Direction and Illustrations by
Elena T. Ivy

Another "Learn about Texas" publication from
TEXAS PARKS AND WILDLIFE PRESS
ISBN - 1-885696-36-1

© 2001 Texas Parks and Wildlife
4200 Smith School Road
Austin, Texas 78744

PWD BK K0700-717

Table of Contents

What, exactly, is a Fish?   1
The Place of Fishes in the Animal Kingdom   2
The Relationships of the Different Groups of Fishes   3
Taxonomy, or How Fishes Get Their Scientific Names   4
The External Parts of Fishes   5
The Internal Parts of Fishes   7
Fish Senses   10
How Fishes Swim   14
How and What Fishes Eat   14
How Fishes Reproduce   16
How Fishes Develop   18
The Origin of Fishes   19
Ancient Jawless Fishes — Ostracoderms   20
Modern Jawless Fishes — Lampreys and Hagfishes   21
First Fishes with Jaws — Acanthodians and Placoderms   22
Cartilaginous Fishes — Sharks, Rabbitfishes and Rays   24
Bony Fishes — Masters of the Water — Lungfishes, Lobe-finned Fishes and Ray-finned Fishes   26
Fish Families.   30 - 80

  Jawless Fishes - Class Agnatha: Lampreys — Family Petromyzontidae   30
  Bony Fishes - Class Osteichthyes: Sturgeons — Family Acipenseridae   31
                                      Paddlefish — Family Polyodontidae   32
                                      Gars — Family Lepisosteidae   33
                                      Bowfins — Family Amiidae   35
                                      Freshwater Eels — Family Anguillidae   36
                                      Herrings and Shads — Family Clupeidae   37
                                      Mooneyes — Family Hiodontidae   38
                                      Trouts, Salmons, Chars and Whitefish — Family Salmonidae   39
                                      Pikes and Pickerels — Family Esocidae   40
                                      Characins — Family Characidae   41
                                      Minnows — Family Cyprinidae   42
                                      Suckers — Family Catostomidae   51
                                      Bullhead Catfishes — Family Ictaluridae   54
                                      Suckermouth Catfishes — Family Loricariidae   57
                                      Pirate Perch — Family Aphredoderidae   58
                                      Topminnows and Killifishes — Family Fundulidae   59
                                      Pupfishes — Family Cyprinodontidae   62
                                      Livebearers — Family Poeciliidae   64
                                      Silversides — Family Atherinidae   66
                                      Temperate Basses — Family Moronidae   67
                                      Sunfishes and Basses — Family Centrarchidae   69
                                      Perches, Darters, Walleye and Sauger — Family Percidae   74
                                      Drums or Croakers — Family Sciaenidae   79
                                      Cichlids — Family Cichlidae   80

Table of Contents

Activity Pages

Box Puzzles — 34 - 61

Fish Seek and Find — 81

Make Sunfish Chowder — 82

Get Aquatic WILD, take them Fishing. — 83

Make a Mini-Minnow Mobile — 84

Design a Fish — 85

Place the Fish in the Fish Bowl — 86

Make a Paper Aquarium for White Bass — 87

Fish in a Jar — 88

Fishing Word Puzzle — 89

A fish is a water-living animal with a backbone. It swims with the help of fins. It uses gills to extract oxygen from the surrounding water.

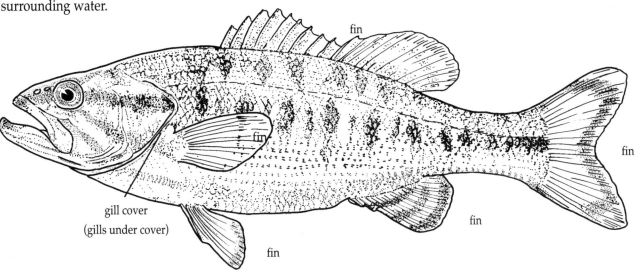

fin

fin

fin

gill cover
(gills under cover)

fin

fin

There are other aquatic backboned animals with fins. Examples are whales and dolphins. However, these are mammals that have adapted to a water-living existence. Their front fins are actually "changed-over" arms, and they breathe (take in oxygen) by inhaling air into their lungs. Also, unlike fishes, these mammals suckle their young with milk.

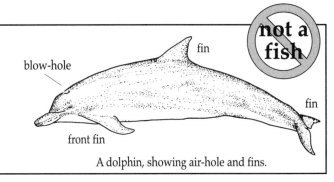

not a fish

blow-hole

fin

fin

front fin

A dolphin, showing air-hole and fins.

Fishes come in many shapes and sizes:

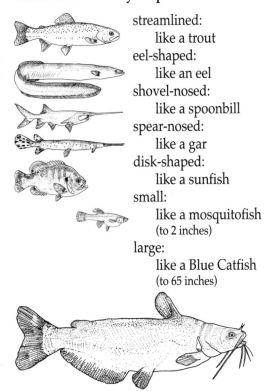

streamlined:
   like a trout
eel-shaped:
   like an eel
shovel-nosed:
   like a spoonbill
spear-nosed:
   like a gar
disk-shaped:
   like a sunfish
small:
   like a mosquitofish
   (to 2 inches)
large:
   like a Blue Catfish
   (to 65 inches)

Where they live:

Some fishes live only in the ocean, while others are strictly freshwater dwellers. Still others go back and forth (migrate) between fresh and salt water. Some of these spend their early years in the ocean and then return to the river or stream where they were born to mate and lay eggs. Salmon are an example. Others, like some eels, spend most of their lives in fresh water and migrate to the ocean for mating and egg-laying. The adults then die and the hatched young return to fresh water.

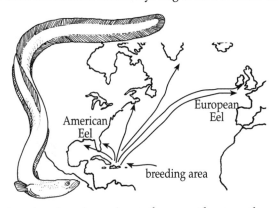

American Eel

European Eel

breeding area

Freshwater eels mate and reproduce in the ocean. The young then return to streams and rivers.

The Place of Fishes in the Animal Kingdom

The animal kingdom is divided into 20 major groupings called **phyla** (singular: phylum). Backboned animals or vertebrates are a subgroup of a phylum called **Chordata** or chordates. The other phyla are popularly lumped together as the invertebrates. [However, remember that each phylum among the invertebrates is quite distinct. Thus the phylum Mollusca (clams, snails, etc.), for example, is as separate from the phylum Echinodermata (starfishes, sea-urchins, etc.) as either of those groups is from the Chordata.]

Phyla, in turn, are divided into groups called **classes**. The **aquatic, gill-breathing, finned vertebrates** are often lumped together as the **Class Pisces** (fishes) as distinguished from the Class Amphibia (amphibians — frogs, toads and salamanders), the Class Reptilia (reptiles — turtles, lizards, snakes, crocodiles and alligators), the Class Aves (birds) and the Class Mammalia (mammals).

Actually, however, the gill-breathing finned vertebrates include a number of very different groups. Most experts, therefore, prefer to label these distinctive groups as separate classes of vertebrates.

Among living fishes, the **bony fishes** or Class Osteichthyes (ost-ay-ick-thees) and the **cartilaginous fishes** or Class Chondrichthyes (con-drick-thees) are the most important. The bony fishes include just about all the fishes you know, with the exception of the sharks and rays which form the cartilaginous class of fishes. There are also the **jawless fishes** forming the Class Agnatha (ag-nay-tha). The only living species belonging to this class are the lampreys and hagfishes. There are two other classes of fishes — the placoderms (Class Placodermi) and the acanthodians (Class Acanthodii) — whose members are all extinct. (see page 22).

Experts estimate that there are about 25,000 species of fishes of which 790 species are known from the fresh waters of the United States and Canada. Texas has 174 of these species.

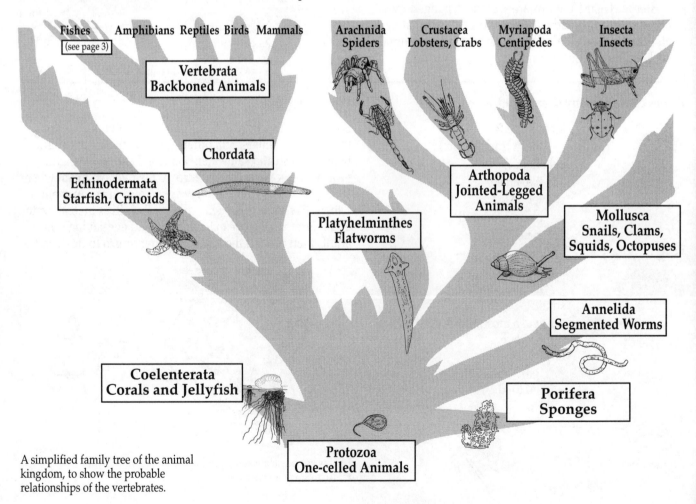

A simplified family tree of the animal kingdom, to show the probable relationships of the vertebrates.

The Relationships of the Different Groups of Fishes

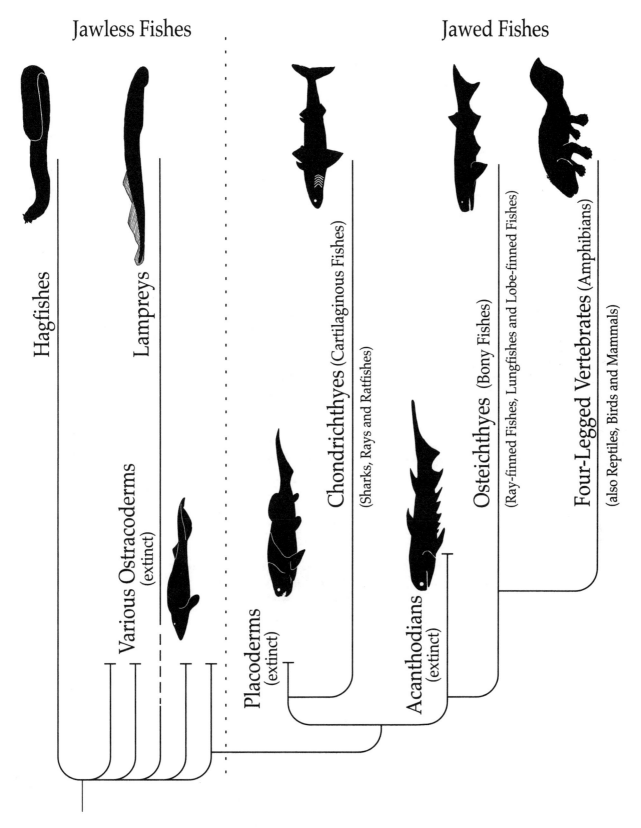

Jawless Fishes

Jawed Fishes

Hagfishes

Lampreys

Various Ostracoderms (extinct)

Placoderms (extinct)

Chondrichthyes (Cartilaginous Fishes)
(Sharks, Rays and Ratfishes)

Acanthodians (extinct)

Osteichthyes (Bony Fishes)
(Ray-finned Fishes, Lungfishes and Lobe-finned Fishes)

Four-Legged Vertebrates (Amphibians)
(also Reptiles, Birds and Mammals)

Only hagfishes and lampreys survive from among the ancient jawless fishes. Cartilaginous and bony fishes include the vast majority of living forms. Four-legged vertebrates are an offshoot from certain extinct bony fishes. (See pages 19 - 29 for details).

Taxonomy
or How Fishes Get their Scientific Names

Scientists have developed a system into which all living things (organisms) can be placed and then given a scientific name. This system is called **taxonomy** and it consists of "higher" and "lower" groups. The higher the group, the more broad it is — meaning that it contains a wider range of organisms than the group below it. Let's see how this system works for fishes, let's say, specifically, the Guadalupe bass.

To fit this particular fish into the topmost level, we need to place it into one of five divisions called **kingdoms**. Animals, plants, fungi, bacteria and one-celled organisms each have their own kingdom. The Guadalupe bass is obviously an animal, hence it belongs in the Kingdom Animalia (Latin for "animal").

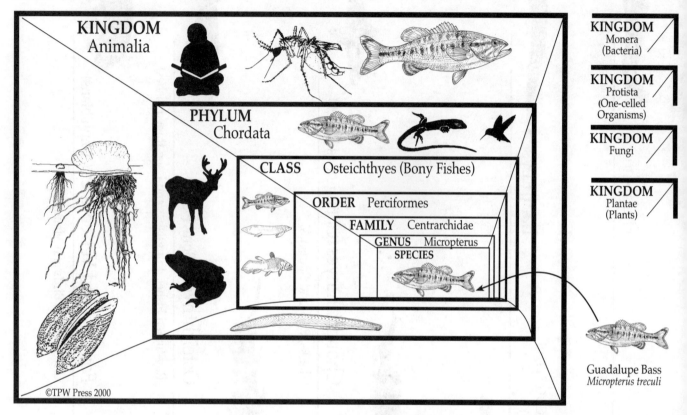

KINGDOM Animalia · PHYLUM Chordata · CLASS Osteichthyes (Bony Fishes) · ORDER Perciformes · FAMILY Centrarchidae · GENUS Micropterus · SPECIES

KINGDOM Monera (Bacteria) · KINGDOM Protista (One-celled Organisms) · KINGDOM Fungi · KINGDOM Plantae (Plants)

Guadalupe Bass
Micropterus treculi

©TPW Press 2000

KINGDOM ANIMALIA (ah-nee-mah-lee-ah) contains: coelenterates (jellyfish, etc.), echinoderms (starfish, etc.), flatworms, segmented worms, mollusks, jointed-legged animals (insects, etc.), and *chordates* . Each of these groups is called a **phylum**. Among animals, fishes belong with the phylum chordates (called Chordata in Latin) which includes all the backboned animals.

PHYLUM CHORDATA (kor-dah-tah) contains: vertebrates or backboned animals, along with other chordates without backbones such as lancelets. Vertebrates consist of 7 living classes: Jawless Fishes (Agnatha), Cartilaginous Fishes (Chondrichthyes), Bony Fishes (Osteichthyes), Amphibians, Reptiles, Birds and Mammals.

CLASS Osteichthyes (ost-ay-ick-thees) contains: bony fishes, or all the living fishes other than sharks, rays, lampreys and hagfishes. There are 45 orders of bony fishes.

ORDER PERCIFORMES (per-see-form-ease) contains: some 200 families of advanced bony fishes (the teleosts) such as perches, porgies, remoras, angelfish, cichlids, wrasses, gobies, mullets, mackerels, barracudas, gouramis and members of the family Centrarchidae.

FAMILY CENTRARCHIDAE (sen-trar-key-day) contains: black basses, sunfishes and crappies, some 30 species in all.

GENUS *MICROPTERUS* (my-krop-ter-us) meaning "small fin" contains 7 species of basses often called "black basses" because of their overall dark color. In Texas, this genus contains the Guadalupe bass, largemouth bass, smallmouth bass and spotted bass.

SPECIES *MICROPTERUS TRECULI* (tre-cue-lie) contains the Guadalupe bass. This is the species name, made up of two names: the genus name first and then the specific name second. In this case *Micropterus* and *treculi*. Both are always italicized, with the genus name spelled with a capital.

Only the anatomy of **ray-finned bony fishes** (see page 26) will be discussed since all of Texas' freshwater species, except for the jawless lampreys, belong to this subgroup of bony fishes.

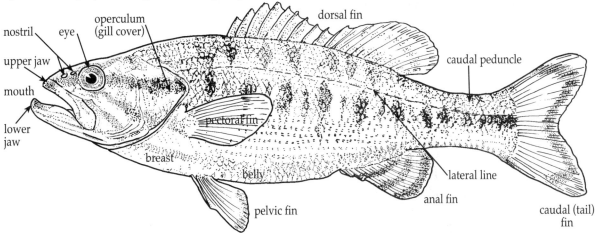

Fins

Fishes have two sets of paired fins. The **pectoral fins** are located on the lower half of the body directly behind the head. The **pelvic fins** are usually located further back on the belly. (The more "advanced" the fish, the more forward in placement the pelvic fins, and the higher up on the body the pectoral fins become.)

Fishes also have three unpaired fins. Along the back is the **dorsal fin** (often divided into two parts, one behind the other). The tail fin is called the **caudal fin.** The **anal fin** is located on the underside of the fish in front of the tail fin.

Lateral-Line System

This is a long canal, usually below the scales, with pores placed at regular intervals, running the length of either side of the fish. The canal is lined with special sensory structures for detecting vibrations (see page 12).

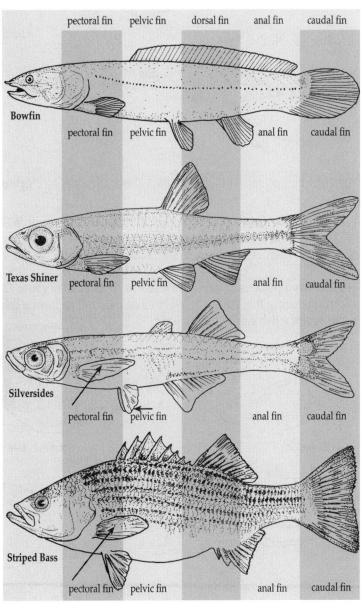

Head

There are two **eyes**, a **mouth** opening framed by an upper and lower jaw, **nostrils** consisting of two openings on each side, and a skin-covered bony flap called the **operculum** covering the gill slits. If you turn back the loose hind edge of the operculum you can see the gill arches (see pages 7, 15). The front sides of the frontmost gill arches have comb-like "teeth" called **gill rakers**. The back side of each gill arch carries the filament-like gills.

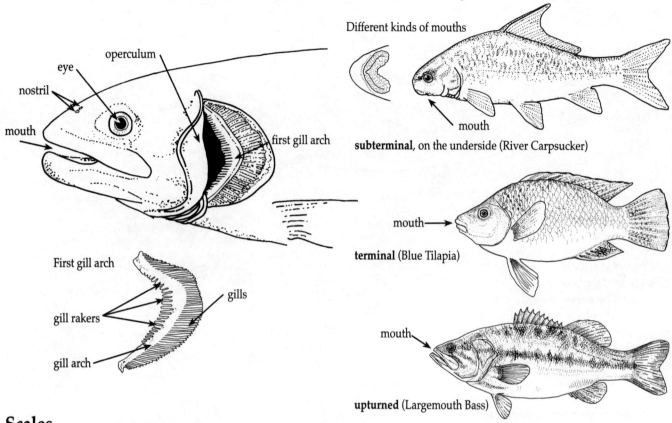

Different kinds of mouths

eye
operculum
nostril
mouth
first gill arch

subterminal, on the underside (River Carpsucker)

First gill arch
gill rakers
gills
gill arch

mouth
terminal (Blue Tilapia)

mouth
upturned (Largemouth Bass)

Scales

All freshwater bony fishes develop scales after hatching. Primitive fishes like gars (see page 33) have heavy, platelike scales called **ganoid** scales. Those of more advanced fishes are much thinner. Such thin scales can be comblike along the edges. They are then called **ctenoid**. Thin scales can also be smooth-edged or **cycloid**.

Scales grow from pockets in the skin and form **rings** as they grow. During the cold months, growth slows down and the rings formed during this season are very close together to form a thick **annual ring**. By counting the number of annual rings, the age of a fish can be determined.

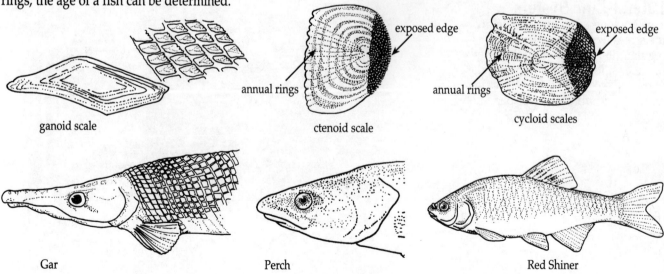

ganoid scale

exposed edge
annual rings
ctenoid scale

exposed edge
annual rings
cycloid scales

Gar

Perch

Red Shiner

The internal structure of ray-finned bony fishes follows the basic vertebrate plan. [With variations, this plan is common to fishes in general, as well as amphibians, reptiles, birds and mammals, including humans.]

Specifically, ray-finned bony fishes have the following internal parts:

1) An **internal support system** called a **skeleton,** including a jointed series of disc-shaped bony structures called **vertebrae** running down the back; **ribs** arising from the vertebrae; **fin supports**; and a rigid head skeleton called a **skull** made up of many bones including a braincase.

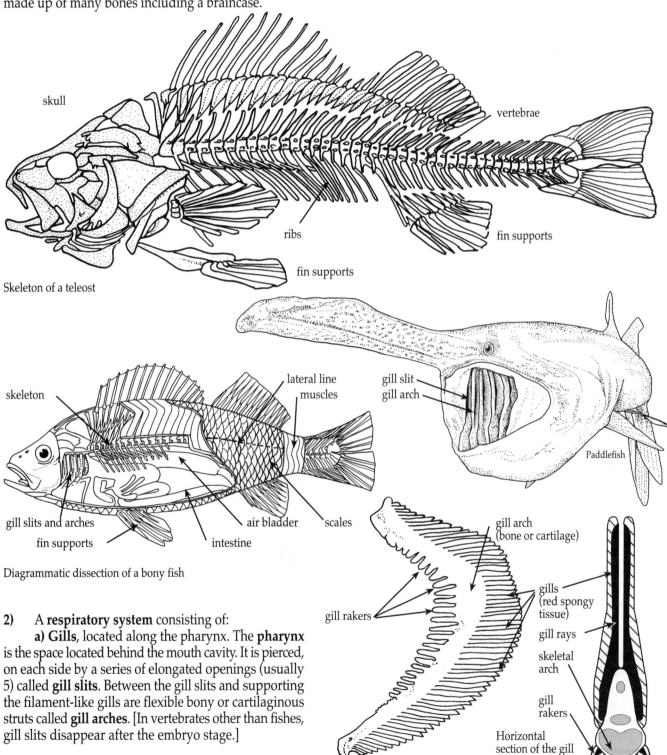

Skeleton of a teleost

Diagrammatic dissection of a bony fish

2) A **respiratory system** consisting of:
a) Gills, located along the pharynx. The **pharynx** is the space located behind the mouth cavity. It is pierced, on each side by a series of elongated openings (usually 5) called **gill slits**. Between the gill slits and supporting the filament-like gills are flexible bony or cartilaginous struts called **gill arches**. [In vertebrates other than fishes, gill slits disappear after the embryo stage.]

Horizontal section of the gill arch of a teleost

b) Lungs. Some bony fishes, like the lungfishes (see page 27) and a few primitive ray-finned bony fishes (see page 29) also have lungs in addition to gills. In the vast majority of ray-fins, however, air-breathing lungs have disappeared. Instead, a sac-shaped structure called an **air-bladder** has taken their place. The air-bladder lies above and is connected to the digestive tube. Filling or emptying the air in the air-bladder helps the fish rise up or go down in the water.

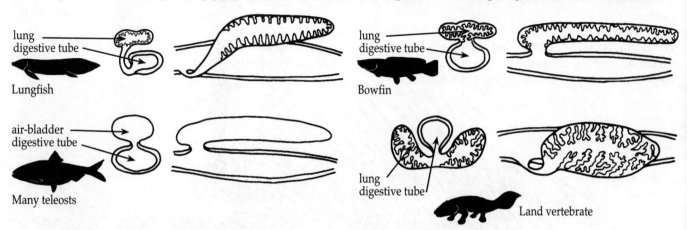

3) A **muscular system** consisting of:

a) Trunk muscles, made up of segmented muscles that contract in waves and throw the body of the fish into S-shaped curves [each muscle segment is shaped like a **W** on its side], (see Fish Movement page 14).

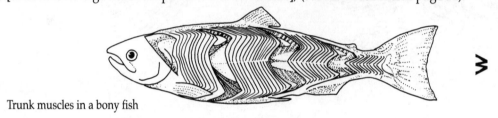

Trunk muscles in a bony fish

b) Branchial muscles that cause the pharynx to expand, pumping water across the gill filaments. The muscles that move the jaws are specialized branchial muscles. [In vertebrates with legs, some of the trunk muscles become limb muscles and the branchial muscles serve as face, neck and shoulder muscles.]

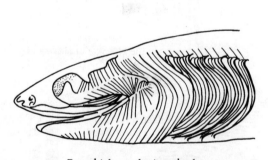

Branchial muscles in a shark

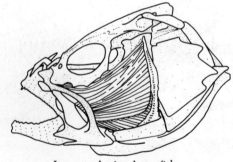

Jaw muscles in a bony fish

4) A **digestive system** consisting of a tube (called the **intestinal tract**) leading from mouth to anus. Food travels from one end to the other. After passing through the pharynx, food enters the **oesophagus** (ease-o-fa-gus), then a storage and grinding-up pouch called the **stomach** and, finally, the **intestine** where and from which most of digestion and absorption into the blood stream takes place. Where stomach and intestine join there are usually finger-like outgrowths.

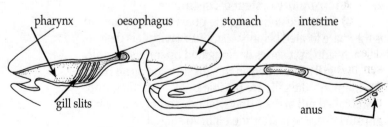

Digestive system of an advanced bony fish

5) A **urinary** (or **excretory**) **system**, made up of a pair of **kidneys** and their ducts for conducting urine to the outside. The kidneys filter waste products from the bloodstream and in bony fishes excrete them as ammonia. (In most freshwater fishes part of this ammonia is excreted by the way of the gills.)

6) A **reproductive system** which differs depending on the sex of the fish.

Males have a pair of sex glands called **testes**. These produce sperm which is released to the outside by ducts during mating (see Reproduction page 16). Females have paired sex glands called **ovaries**. The eggs are usually conducted to the outside and fertilized by the sperm during mating. The urinary and reproductive systems are closely linked in vertebrates and are often called the **urogenital system**.

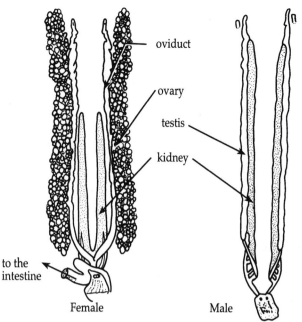

The urinary and reproductive system of a lungfish are closely linked (as in all vertebrates).

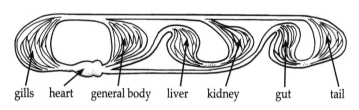

Blood circulation network of a typical fish

7) A closed **circulatory system** along which blood is pumped by a two-chambered **heart**. Arteries conduct oxygen-rich blood from the gills to all the cells in the body. Veins then collect the now oxygen-poor blood from various parts of the body organs and lead it back to the gills to be filled with oxygen again.

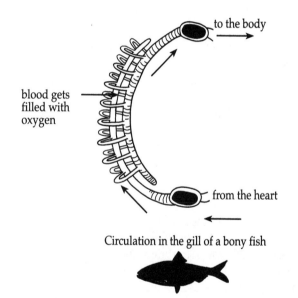

Circulation in the gill of a bony fish

8) A **central nervous system** made up of a hollow nerve cord that runs down the back (above the backbone). This **spinal cord** becomes enlarged in the head region where it forms the **brain**. Nerves emerge from the spinal cord at each segment of the body along the way. These nerves enable the fish to feel body sensations and to contract its trunk muscles. Special nerves called cranial nerves are connected to the brain, supplying various sense organs, the pharynx and organs located farther down in the body.

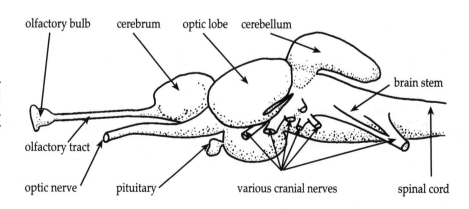

Side view of the brain of a codfish

Fish Senses

Like all animals, fishes sense the world around them in different ways. But not only do they have the familiar senses of **touch**, **vision**, **hearing**, **smell** and **taste**, they also have a sense for detecting water movements in their surroundings. And, some fishes even have a sense for detecting electrical currents.

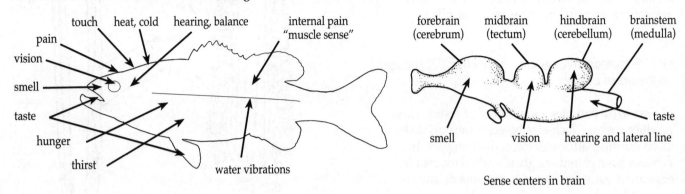

Sense centers in brain

Vision or the perception of light is called **photoreception**. Hearing, the sense of equilibrium and the detection of water vibrations in fishes all depend on sensing mechanical vibrations and are therefore considered forms of **mechanoreception**. Smell and taste both depend on the detection of chemicals and are therefore considered forms of **chemoreception**. Peculiar to certain fishes is the ability to sense minute electrical currents in water. This is called **electroreception**.

Touch and Other "Simple" Senses

All animals respond to touch or pressure. In fishes, sensations of touch are the result of direct stimulation of the free end fibers of the sensory nerves scattered throughout the skin. Nerve endings in the skin also register sensations of pain as well as heat and cold, to all of which fishes are known to respond. We also know from ourselves that there are sensory structures that inform us about the tenseness of our muscles ("muscle sense"), the motion of our joints, hunger, thirst, internal pain and many other sensations. Fishes must also have such internal receptors. Otherwise they could not adequately meet the various demands of their environment.

Vision — Photoreception

In fishes, as in all vertebrates, the organs concerned with vision are the eyes, located on either side of the head. Each eye consists of an **eyeball**, situated in a recess, called the **orbit**, on the side of the braincase. The eye is connected to the brain by the stalk-like **optic nerve** that comes out from behind the eye. Inside the hollow eyeball are two chambers, filled with gelatinous liquids. Located towards the front, in between the two chambers, lies a spherical (round) lens suspended by ligaments and muscles.

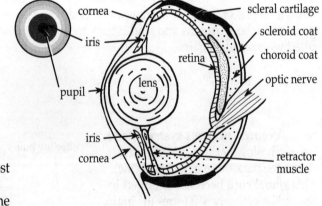

Typical fish eye structure

The walls of the eyeball are formed by three layers. The innermost layer is the light-sensitive **retina**, which is incomplete near the front. The cells making up the retina contain pigments that become bleached out when exposed to light. This stimulates the cells and they send signals, by way of the optic nerve, to the brain. The brain then interprets the patterns or images registered on the retina. Most teleost fishes (like some other vertebrates) have two kinds of retinal cells, called **rods** and **cones**. Both kinds perceive images in black and white, but cone cells are specialized to see in color. Behind the retina, is the middle layer of the eyeball, called the **choroid coat**. Its function is to supply food and oxygen by way of tiny blood vessels. The choroid layer, like the retina, is incomplete in front. The retina and choroid fuse up front to form lens-suspending ligaments and muscles and also a structure called the **iris**. In fishes, the round lens sticks out from a hole (called the **pupil**) in the iris.

The outermost layer, called the **scleroid coat,** is protective in function. Unlike the other two layers, it is complete around the eyeball. The scleroid coat is transparent in front (where it is called the **cornea**) so that light can enter the lens. Around the sides, the scleroid coat is hardened with cartilage and bone for good support of the eyeball.

In teleosts and lampreys, accommodation, or focusing of the image, is brought about by moving the lens backward. In its ordinary position, the lens is focused for near vision, while distance vision requires pulling the lens back with special muscles. (The shark lens, by the way, works in just the opposite fashion: near vision requires moving the lens forward from its relaxed position.)

Mechanoreception

In fishes, mechanoreception includes the **perception of water vibrations**, the sensing of sounds (**hearing**) and the sense of **orientation** or balance. Hearing and orientation occur in the inner ear, while water vibrations are detected by the external lateral-line system. Mechanoreception depends on the mechanical bending of hairs on sensory cells by the movement of fluids. The bending of hair cells happens inside the inner ear during hearing and orientation, while sensing water vibrations involves hair cells that are distorted inside special canals along the fish's skin surface. The structures responsible for all mechanoreception are called **neuromasts.** Each neuromast consists of a cluster of cells with hairs that point upward and which are enclosed in a jelly-filled dome called a **cupula**. The movement of fluids pushes the cupula and with it the enclosed sensory hairs, setting off nerve impulses that are relayed to the brain. The neuromast structure is typical of the lateral-line system. It becomes variously modified in the inner ear for hearing and for balance.

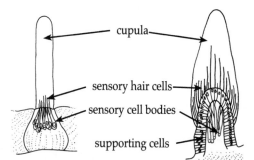

cupula

sensory hair cells
sensory cell bodies
supporting cells

Typical neuromast in skin

Modified neuromast inside a semicircular canal of the inner ear

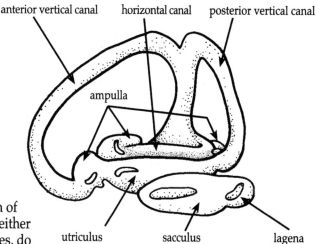

anterior vertical canal   horizontal canal   posterior vertical canal

ampulla

utriculus   sacculus   lagena

The three semicircular canals and utriculus function for balance and gravity detection. The sacculus and lagena function for hearing.

Hearing

In fishes, as with all vertebrates, hearing, or the detection of sound vibrations, takes place in the inner ear located on either side of the braincase. Fishes, unlike land-going vertebrates, do not have a middle ear or an external ear like mammals. The inner ear of fishes, again as with all vertebrates, consists of a complex fluid-filled membranous structure. The upper portion of the structure is made up of three small semicircular canals opening into a sac called the **utriculus** (you-trick-you-lus) located below them. This upper portion functions for equilibrium and gravity detection (see page 12). In fishes the lower portion consists of a sac called the **sacculus** (sack-uh-lus). A bulging portion of the sacculus to one side is called the **lagena** (la-gee-nah). Sound detection in fish is accomplished in the sacculus and the lagena. Both have patches of sensory hair cells. In both areas, the combined tips of these cells are surrounded by a jelly-like **cupula** (which in ray-finned fishes becomes filled with calcium deposits and changed into an **otolith** or ear stone). The saccular otolith of teleosts fills almost the entire sacculus and is so species specific that scientists can use it to identify the fish it came from.

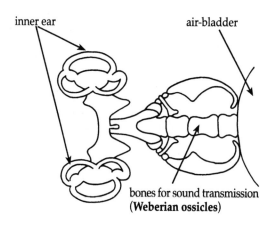

inner ear   air-bladder

bones for sound transmission
(**Weberian ossicles**)

Sounds travel well in water. (Actually five times faster than in air.) As sound waves reach the fish's body, the fluid-suspended otoliths inside the sacculus and the lagena begin to move, bending the protruding hairs of the sensory cells. This nervous stimulation is transmitted to the main acoustic nerve and on into the acoustic lobe of the brain, where sound reception occurs. Sensitivity of hearing is increased by the gas bubble in the air-bladder of fishes. This bubble pulsates when exposed to sound waves causing the bladder wall to vibrate. The air-bladder vibration is then passed to the inner ear. Some fishes have special air-bladder extensions that actually touch the inner ear. Others, like carp and catfish, connect the air-bladder to the inner ear with a chain of small bones called Weberian ossicles.

Equilibrium and Balance

The three semicircular canals and the sac-like utriculus below them are the inner ear structures concerned with balance and spatial orientation.

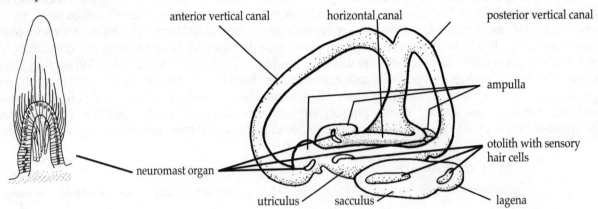

Each of the three canals lies in a plane at right angles to the other two. That way, one canal is present for each of the planes in space. Two canals are in vertical planes and one canal is horizontal. Each canal has an expanded portion near the base called an ampulla (am-pew-la). Each ampulla contains a modified neuromast organ consisting of a cluster of sensory cells whose hairs protrude into a jelly-filled cupula. The utriculus, like the sacculus below it, contains a patch with an otolith. As the fish swims and turns, displacement of liquid inside the canals and in the utriculus displaces the ampullar cupulas and the utricular otolith so that sensory hair cells are mechanically stimulated. The fish is thus informed of its turning movements (angular acceleration) in the three dimensions of space and also, by way of the utriculus, of its straight-line acceleration and deceleration.

Lateral-Line System

This is a sensory system designed to detect water vibrations, such as currents and other disturbances, in contact with the fish's body. A main element of the system is the lateral line as such. This is a long canal, usually below the scales, with pores placed at regular intervals, running the length of either side of the fish. The canal continues onto the head where it branches into a complex pattern of similar canals.

The receptors of this system are the neuromast organs mentioned earlier, (see page 11). The neuromasts line the canal at regular intervals. (Some fishes also have individual neuromasts located in pits scattered over the head and body.) As water flows through the canals in one direction or another, the jelly-like cupulas into which the neuromast cells protrude are bent and so are the sensory hairs. Nervous impulses from these cells are then relayed to the brain and let the fish know the direction of the water disturbance. Some killifish (see page 59) have head neuromasts that sense the surface ripples from struggling insects. Certain blind cavefishes use their head neuromasts, arranged in ridges, to find their prey.

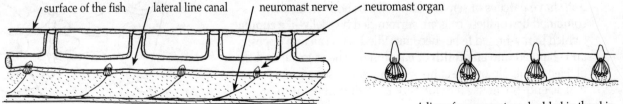

A line of neuromasts embedded in the skin

Longitudinal section through a lateral line canal of a fish

Smell and Taste — Chemoreception

We and other land-based vertebrates have no problem distinguishing between smell and taste. **Olfaction**, or the sense of smell, is stimulated by chemicals in the air carried to special nerve cells in our nostrils. **Taste**, on the other hand, depends on receptors in the mouth in contact with weak solutions of various substances. In fishes, however, both smell and taste receptors pick up, through direct contact, chemicals dissolved in water. The two senses are distinguished in fishes by where on the body the chemoreceptors are located, as well as the part of the brain that the sensory nerve fibers lead to for processing.

Olfaction or Smell

In fishes the smell receptors are located in the olfactory pits, one on each side of the head. Each pit has two external openings through which water flows in and out. Motion of the water through the pit is maintained by the waving of tiny hairs on the cells lining the pit and also by the force of the fish's moving forward through the water. Dissolved chemicals make contact with a pleated surface rich in olfactory nerve endings. Unlike other sensory nerves in vertebrates, the olfactory receptors conduct their impulses directly to the brain without any nerve relays in-between, as is the case for all the other senses (vision, hearing, etc.). The portion of the brain that receives the smell impulses is called the olfactory bulb located at the very front of the brain. (There are two olfactory bulbs, one for each olfactory pit.)

The more important the sense of smell is to a given species of fish, the larger the surface devoted to smell nerves in the olfactory pits and the larger the "smell information" centers in the brain. Eels and sharks have "oversized" olfactory bulbs for smell information processing.

Taste

Taste is an important source of information for identifying food as well as harmful substances. Unlike smell receptors which are located in a fish's olfactory pits, sensory nerves for taste perception, called taste buds, are located in the mouth, the palate and the pharynx as well as on various body surfaces, fins and fleshy head tentacles called barbels. Bottom-dwelling species, such as catfishes, all have barbels.

The pelvic fins of some gouramis and the rostrum (pointed head end) of sturgeons are also lined with taste buds. The protruding lips of certain minnows, too, are well equipped with taste sensors. Sensations of taste from the mouth and pharynx go to the hindmost section of the brain (called the **medulla**), for processing, while tastes from the skin go to a brain area located farther forward.

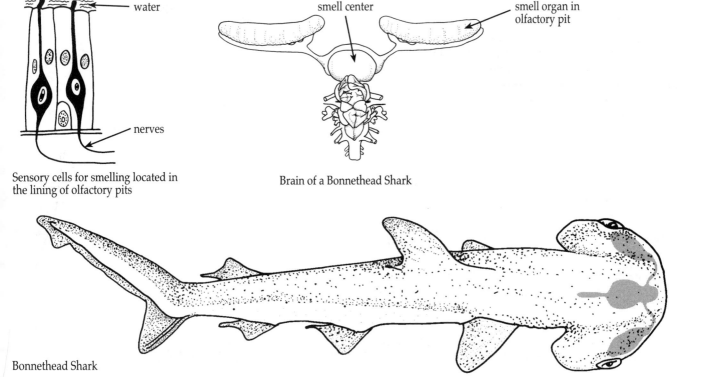

water

nerves

Sensory cells for smelling located in the lining of olfactory pits

smell center

smell organ in olfactory pit

Brain of a Bonnethead Shark

Bonnethead Shark

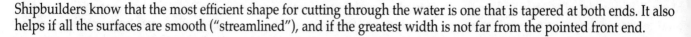

How Fishes Swim

Shipbuilders know that the most efficient shape for cutting through the water is one that is tapered at both ends. It also helps if all the surfaces are smooth ("streamlined"), and if the greatest width is not far from the pointed front end.

Most actively swimming fishes follow this model, as do the mammals (whales) and reptiles (extinct ichthyosaurs) that have taken to a fully water-adapted existence.

In general, too, the back part of the fish body is flattened from side to side. This oar-like flattening has to do with how fish use their bodies for pushing themselves through the water. Fishes move forward by side-to-side movements brought about by waves of muscle contractions that run down the body, first on one side, then the other.

As successive waves travel backward along the trunk and tail, the body as a whole is thrust forward. The flexible yet stiff backbone provides resistance so that the body bends from side to side rather than being shortened up.

Thus, the main thrust is from the power transmitted to the tail (or caudal) fin. In advanced ray-fins (the teleosts, see page 29) this fin is symmetrical and strengthened with special bony supports attached to the end of the backbone.

However, most early or archaic fishes (see placoderms, acanthodians, chondrosteans) have an asymmetrical tail called a **heterocercal** tail. Here the tip of the body turns upward into the tail, and the majority of the fin membrane is located below this fleshy lobe. The function of such a tail is to push the body upward while swimming. Once the air-bladder developed in the teleosts, however, the heterocercal tail was no longer necessary for providing lift. [Sharks still have an heterocercal tail probably because they never developed an air-bladder.]

The forward-pushing movements of the fish's side-to-side muscle contractions would not be very effective, however, without median and paired fins. Fins help in stabilizing and in steering. Rolling motions are checked mainly by the median fins (the dorsal above and the anal below). The paired fins, especially the pectorals, are used mainly for steering, backing up and sometimes for "rowing" the fish forward. Some fishes can even rotate their paired fins, not just move them back and forth from the body. The forward-positioning of the paired fins in advanced teleosts (see page 5) lets these fishes move around more efficiently in the water.

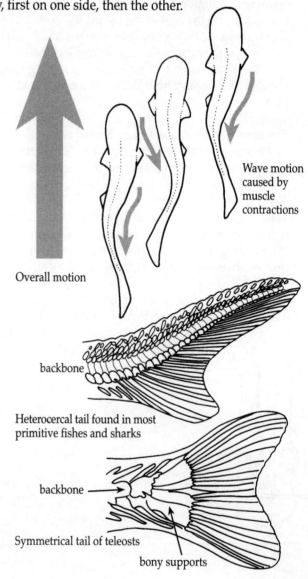

Wave motion caused by muscle contractions

Overall motion

backbone

Heterocercal tail found in most primitive fishes and sharks

backbone

Symmetrical tail of teleosts

bony supports

 # What and How Fishes Eat

When it comes to feeding, fishes can be classified as:
1) **carnivores** — flesh-eaters (usually other fishes)
2) **herbivores** — plant-eaters (mostly algae)
3) **detritivores** — organic-matter feeders (on plant and animal remains on the bottom)
4) **omnivores** — "everything"-eaters (invertebrates, fish and algae, usually)
5) **planktivores** — plankton-eaters (small floating plants and animals suspended in the water)

Most fishes, no matter what the predominant food item, eat a mixed diet. Also frequently, a given species of fish will eat different foods at different stages of its life. Thus, the young of many fishes feed on plankton but switch to larger food items later in life.

Fishes use three basic methods for obtaining food:

1)   **ram feeding** — involving the overtaking of food items (large or small) by rapidly swimming and then ramming the food, along with the surrounding water, through the open mouth. The water is then pushed out through the open gill covers, leaving anything edible in the mouth cavity or trapped in the gill rakers. Some catfishes feed in this manner.

ram feeding

2)   **manipulation** — involving grasping, biting or scraping food (either plant or animal) with the jaws. Jaws lined with sharp teeth were typical for ancestral bony fishes. Active fish-capturing-and-eating fishes like pike still have such jaws.

manipulation feeding

3)   **suction feeding** — involving quickly opening the jaws to create negative pressure inside the mouth cavity. The resulting inrushing water then carries suspended food items (large or small) with it. Most advanced teleosts (for example, bass) use this method, In these fishes the jaws are shortened and the front portion of the upper jaw (the premaxillary bone) is **protusile**, meaning it can be pushed forward by the toothless maxillary bone behind it.

suction feeding

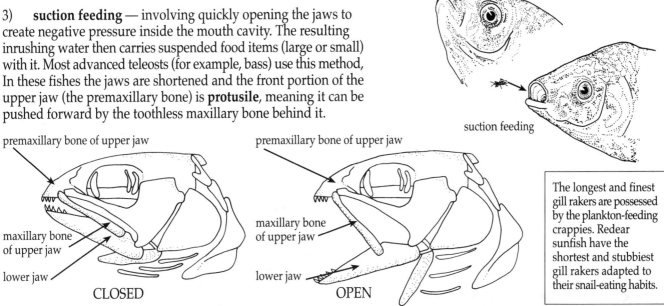

premaxillary bone of upper jaw

premaxillary bone of upper jaw

maxillary bone of upper jaw

lower jaw

CLOSED

maxillary bone of upper jaw

lower jaw

OPEN

The longest and finest gill rakers are possessed by the plankton-feeding crappies. Redear sunfish have the shortest and stubbiest gill rakers adapted to their snail-eating habits.

This mechanism allows for a quick and wide gape and consequent sucking in of water together with any suspended food.

Most advanced teleosts also have **pharyngeal teeth** attached to the fifth gill arch that help in processing the food obtained by suction feeding.

Suction feeding is also ideal for trapping food in the gill area as the sucked-in water is expelled through the gill covers. Consequently, many gill raker specializations can be found among advanced teleosts such as the sunfish family (see page 69). The largemouth bass, for example, has short, widely spaced and pointed gill rakers that can hold on to any fish sucked in and also help in rubbing off its scales before swallowing. No one method is generally used exclusively, and feeding often involves a mixture of all three methods.

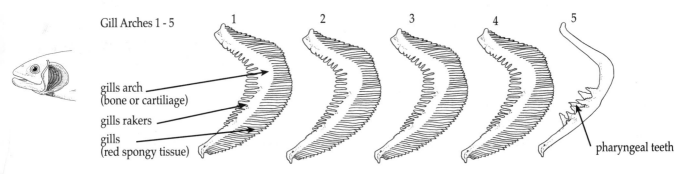

Gill Arches 1 - 5

1   2   3   4   5

gills arch (bone or cartiliage)

gills rakers

gills (red spongy tissue)

pharyngeal teeth

How Fishes Reproduce

In most fish species, males and females appear much alike from the outside. Internally, however, males have a pair of smooth white structures called **testes** or male gonads, while females have a pair of large yellowish granular structures called **ovaries** or female gonads. (See Internal Parts of Fishes, page 9). (During the breeding season ovaries can account for over one-half of the female's weight.) Generally, during mating, sperm (from the testes) and eggs (from the ovaries) are passed to the outside through special pores or ducts. This is called **spawning**. The sperm then fertilizes the eggs which go on to develop first into embryos, then free-swimming larvae and eventually, adults.

A few fishes have **internal fertilization**. Here, the eggs are fertilized internally by way of special structures on the male that conduct the sperm into the interior of the female. Usually such sperm-conducting structures are modified fins. Examples are the **claspers** of sharks and rays formed from the pelvic fins, and the modified anal fins of livebearers (mosquitofish, guppies and mollies, see page 64).

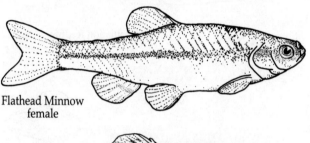

Flathead Minnow
female

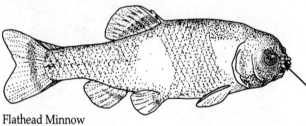

Flathead Minnow
male

In species where males and females do differ externally, the most common difference is in size. Females are generally, but not always, the larger of the two sexes. In some species males sport gaudy colors, especially during the breeding season and sometimes permanently. (Examples can be found among the darters, minnows and sunfishes.)

Males of a few species also have special structures, such as enlarged fins.

A fairly common sexual feature among the males of many fish families are bumps on the head called **breeding tubercles**.

After mating, breeding behavior varies greatly. In general, fishes can be considered either **nonguarders**, **guarders** or **bearers**.

Nonguarders
These fish do not protect their eggs or resulting young once spawning has occurred. Most of the nonguarders swiftly scatter their eggs in the surrounding environment, either open water (many marine species) or on the bottom

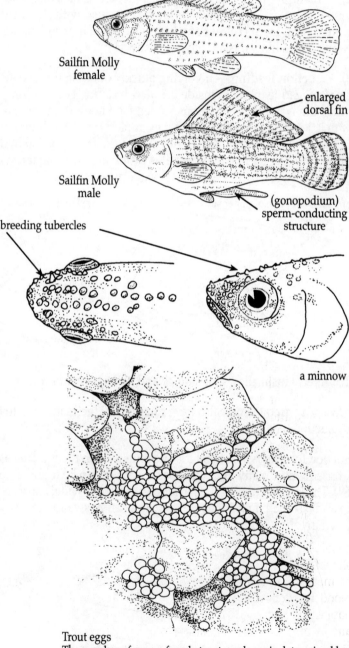

Sailfin Molly
female

enlarged
dorsal fin

Sailfin Molly
male

(gonopodium)
sperm-conducting
structure

breeding tubercles

a minnow

Trout eggs
The number of eggs a female trout produces is determined by her size. An 8-inch fish may lay only 300 eggs, while the nest of a 12-inch fish may contain 1,000 eggs.

(most freshwater species). Some (for example, carp and pike) spawn only in flooded vegetation, where the sticky eggs and embryos remain until the free-moving larvae disperse. In other species (such as trout and minnows) females hide their eggs by excavating depressions on the bottom or building up piles of stones into which the eggs are laid, fertilized by the male, and then buried by the females. During this process, the nests are vigorously defended by the usually brightly colored males, but are then abandoned.

Guarders

Among guarders, the males (except cichlids) protect the eggs and embryos and sometimes even the free-swimming larvae. Protection consists in chasing off predators and in maintaining high-oxygen levels by fanning currents of water across the developing young.

"Guarder" males are often brightly colored and they compete for egg-laying sites to which they then attract females by going through elaborate courtship rituals. Most male "guarders" build pits or depressions (for example, sunfishes and basses) for the female to lay her eggs in, but some just clear off a suitable patch on the bottom. Some species (such as darters and minnows) use natural caves formed by flat rocks or boards for egg-laying and fertilization. Catfish often use hollow logs or empty containers over which the males stand their guard.

Bearers

Bearers are species that carry their developing young around with them, either externally or internally. Generally, the males are the ones that carry young externally. Such males usually have special skin pouches into which the eggs are placed (for example, the marine seahorses). Among cichlids, (see page 80) it is usually the female that picks up the young with her mouth after spawning and carries them in her mouth cavity throughout her young's embryonic development.

In species that are **internal bearers** the eggs are fertilized inside the female and she then carries the developing young inside her body cavity until they are released to the outside, usually as free-swimming larvae. The growing embryos obtain their nourishment either from the egg yolk or from placenta-like structures by means of which nutriments from the mother's bloodstream pass into the embryos. (Similar to what happens in mammals). Many kinds of sharks and rays and members of the live-bearing molly and gambusia family give birth to small broods of young that have developed internally.

Among cichlid mouth brooders, the male displays his brightly marked anal fin to his prospective mate. He swims over a stone that he has cleaned of sand, where the female will lay her eggs. He then fertilizes the eggs.

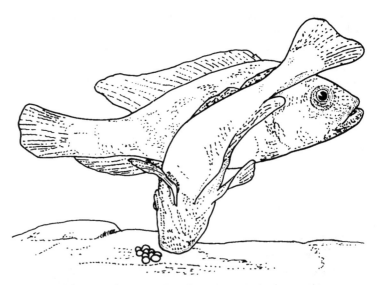

As her mate hovers nearby, the female mouth brooder picks up her newly laid and fertilized eggs. The eggs, which number from 30 to 80, are kept in an extended area of the female's throat sac until ready to hatch.

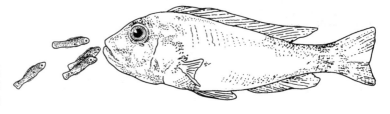

Once they hatch, the young leave their mother's open mouth but stay close by her so that, if danger threatens, they have a handy refuge in their mother's mouth.

17

A fish's development from fertilized egg to eventual old age and death can be broken up into five periods:

1)   **Embryonic period** —This is the time during which the developing fish is entirely dependent on nutrition provided by the mother. This can occur externally or internally by means of the yolk present in the egg, or by an internal placenta-like connection. The embryonic period begins at fertilization and continues through rapid cell divisions until the embryo starts to resemble a fish, inside and out. Most embryos shed their egg membranes and are no longer curled up. However they still draw nourishment from their yolk sac or from the mother's bloodstream.

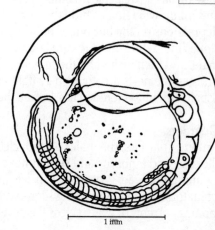

Walleye embryo at 3 days

2)   **Larval period** — The larval period starts when the developing fish can capture its own food. Usually new breathing structures develop at this point. The mouth is now functional and so is the digestive system. This period ends when the backbone is fully formed and separate fins have developed from the single median finfold. Larvae can be either **pelagic** (swimming near the surface) or **benthic** (bottom-living). Lake and river-dwelling freshwater fishes (example sunfishes) usually have pelagic larvae, while stream-dwelling species (like minnows) have larvae that live among the heavy vegetation on the bottom. In live-bearing species, the larval period may be absent or very short (internal).

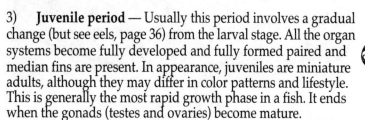

Walleye embryo at 6 days

3)   **Juvenile period** — Usually this period involves a gradual change (but see eels, page 36) from the larval stage. All the organ systems become fully developed and fully formed paired and median fins are present. In appearance, juveniles are miniature adults, although they may differ in color patterns and lifestyle. This is generally the most rapid growth phase in a fish. It ends when the gonads (testes and ovaries) become mature.

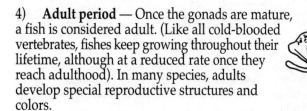

Walleye embryo at 8 days

4)   **Adult period** — Once the gonads are mature, a fish is considered adult. (Like all cold-blooded vertebrates, fishes keep growing throughout their lifetime, although at a reduced rate once they reach adulthood). In many species, adults develop special reproductive structures and colors.

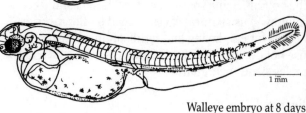

Walleye embryo at 17 days

5)   **Senescent period** — Few individual fishes reach this "old age" stage when growth has virtually stopped and the gonads have begun to degenerate. They usually die, for one reason or another, beforehand. In some species, like sturgeons, this period can last for years.

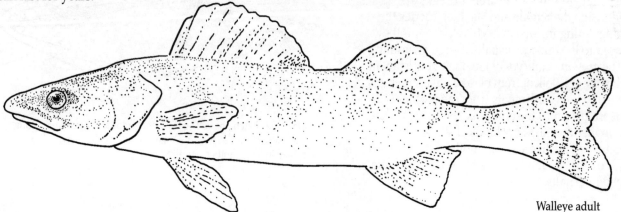

Walleye adult

The Origin of Fishes

The oldest ancestors of fishes are believed to date back to a small worm-like animal called *Pikaia* (Pick-eye-ah) found in rocks about 530 million years old.

Pikaia is the earliest fossil known with an internal front-to-back flexible stiffening rod called a **notochord** and a series of zig-zag muscle blocks along the body. In both these features, *Pikaia* strongly resembles the living **lancelets**, long considered as representative of the kinds of animals with a notochord (the chordates) from which the vertebrates descended.

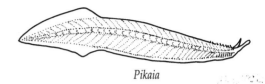

Pikaia

Lancelets live in shallow coastal waters. They burrow in the sand with only their head sticking out. They can swim quite well, however, by S-shaped movements brought about by alternating contractions of the zig-zag body muscles. During these contractions the body is prevented from collapsing upon itself by the flexible notochord.

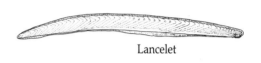

Lancelet

[Fishes swim the same way, except that their notochord becomes surrounded by a series of jointed bony or cartilaginous disks (the **vertebrae**) forming the backbone. That makes fishes not just chordates but **vertebrates**. The notochord is present only during embryonic development in vertebrates; it is replaced by vertebral disks in the adults.]

Lancelets also have many of the same internal structures that fishes and other vertebrates possess. There is a hollow nerve cord located above the notochord. Lancelets have a digestive tube extending from mouth to anus. They also have gill slits. These, however, are very numerous and extend up to half the animal's length. The gills are used not so much for respiration as for filtering organic substances from the water which is drawn in through the mouth. Lancelets also have a closed circulatory system, but no heart.

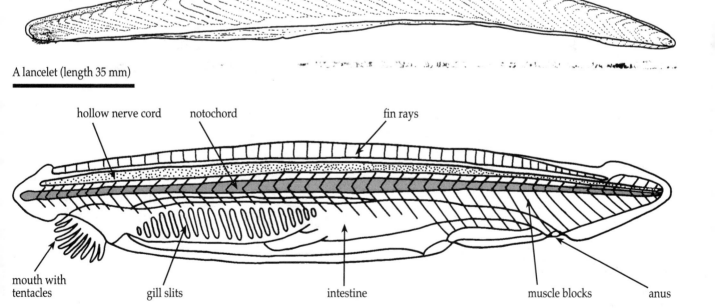

A lancelet (length 35 mm)

Interior structures of a lancelet

The earliest known fishes, dating to some 470 million years ago, were jawless. That means that their mouth openings were not controlled by movements of an upper and lower jaw.

These jawless early fishes are called **ostracoderms** (oh-streh-co-derms). They were the first vertebrates and are believed to be descended from lancelet-like chordates, such as the fossil *Pikaia*, (see page 19).

Most ostracoderms were heavily armored with large and small bony shields covering their body.

Ostracoderms swam by using the motion imparted to their powerful tails by alternating contractions of the muscles along the body. Many of them had median fins on the back or on the underside to prevent rolling. Only a few had paired fins that could be used for steering, however, as in more modern fishes.

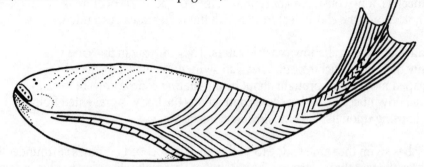

Sacabampasis, from Bolivia, an ostracoderm and the earliest known vertebrate, about 12 inches long.

The rounded or oval mouth opening of ostracoderms was probably used to draw in water (or to suck in mud if the fish was a bottom dweller). Microscopic organisms were then filtered out by straining the water through numerous gill openings.

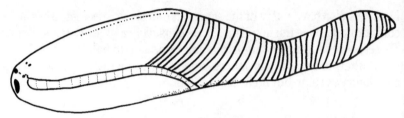

Arandaspis, from Australia, an early ostracoderm, about 8 inches long.

Ostracoderms were quite successful and varied until they died out about 350 million years ago, after the more modern groups of jawed fishes had begun to populate the earth's waters.

Anglaspis, a heavily armored ostracoderm, about 5 inches long.

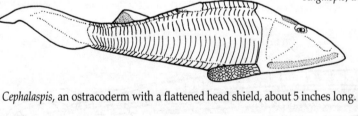

Cephalaspis, an ostracoderm with a flattened head shield, about 5 inches long.

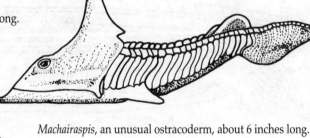

Machairaspis, an unusual ostracoderm, about 6 inches long.

Jamoytius, an unarmored "naked" ostracoderm, about 6 inches long.

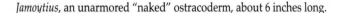

6 inches long.

Two kinds of jawless fishes have continued to exist into modern times. They are the **lampreys** and the **hagfishes**. Both are believed to be descended from some of the ancient ostracoderms. However, they have become greatly altered as an adaptation to the parasitic life-style they have taken up. Both are "naked", resembling in that respect the unarmored ostracoderm **Jaymoytius** (see page 20).

[The extinct ostracoderms, as well as the living lampreys and hagfishes, are placed into the **Class Agnatha**, meaning "jawless ones", in the fish classification used by most biologists.]

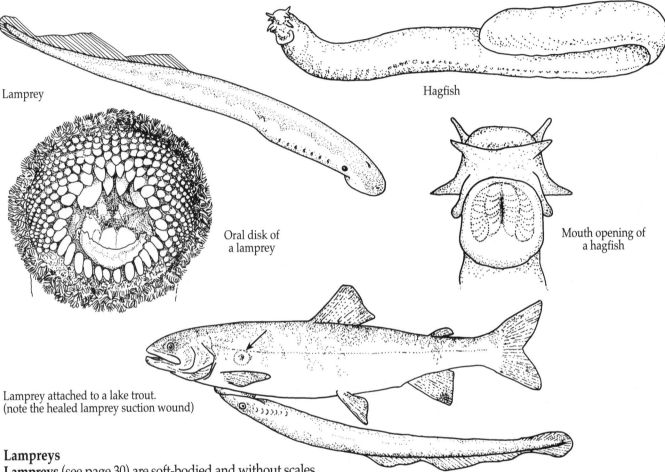

Lamprey

Hagfish

Oral disk of
a lamprey

Mouth opening of
a hagfish

Lamprey attached to a lake trout.
(note the healed lamprey suction wound)

Lampreys
Lampreys (see page 30) are soft-bodied and without scales. They have feeble skeletons made of cartilage, not bone. Along their sides stretch a series of porthole-like gill openings. Most (but not all) lampreys become parasitic as adults when they move from freshwater to large lakes or the ocean. All lampreys start life in freshwater where they hatch as larval forms called **ammocoetes**. These larvae bear a resemblance to lancelets, another argument for thinking of jawless fishes as descendants of the early chordates.

The parasitic adult lampreys use their suckershaped mouth, lined with rasping horny "teeth", to attach themselves to their prey, rasp a hole and suck body fluids.

Hagfishes
The slimy **hagfishes** are even more "degenerate" in their anatomy than the lampreys. They live in the ocean where they attach themselves to and drill their way into dead or dying fishes, in order to eat their flesh and insides. They also feed on invertebrates living on the ocean bottom.

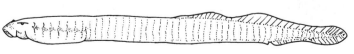

Ammocoete, or lamprey larva.

21

The first jawed fishes appeared about 420 million years ago. Having jaws gave these fishes a big advantage as they could now actively snap up prey, hold it firmly and chew it up. Jawless fishes on the other hand, are limited to being filter-feeders or mudgrubbers like the extinct ostracoderms, or parasites like the modern lampreys.

Biologists believe that paired jaws developed from the frontmost pair of gill arches.

Early jawed fishes are placed into two groups: the **acanthodians** (uh-can-tho-dee-ans) and the **placoderms** (pleh-co-derms).

Acanthodians (Class Acanthodii)
This group's name means "spiny fishes" and with good reason. Acanthodians had a heavy spine in front of their median as well as their paired fins. These fishes were covered in small diamond-shaped scales. In some, only the lower jaw had numerous small teeth; others were toothless.

There were numerous kinds of acanthodians until they died out gradually by 250 million years ago.

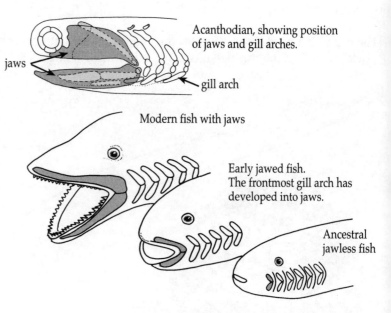

Acanthodian, showing position of jaws and gill arches.

jaws

gill arch

Modern fish with jaws

Early jawed fish. The frontmost gill arch has developed into jaws.

Ancestral jawless fish

Diagram showing how the frontmost gill arch becomes the upper and lower jaws.

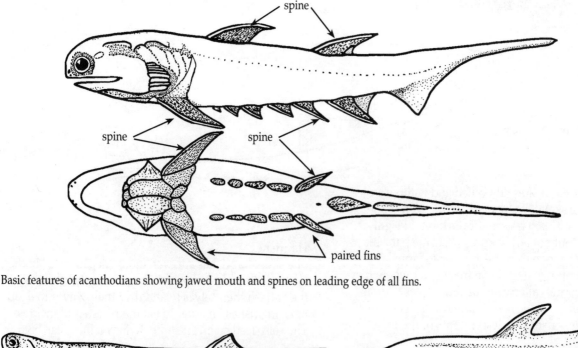

spine

spine

spine

paired fins

Basic features of acanthodians showing jawed mouth and spines on leading edge of all fins.

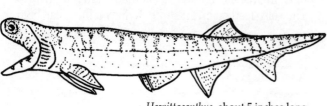

Howittacanthus, about 5 inches long.

Climatius, about 6 inches long.

Two acanthodians

Six different kinds of placoderms

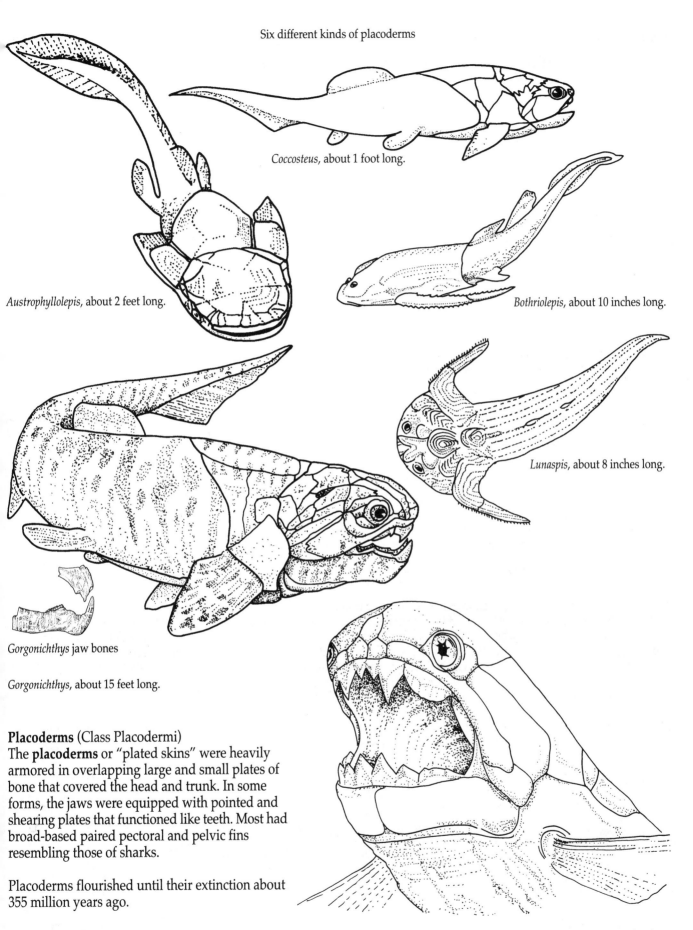

Coccosteus, about 1 foot long.

Austrophyllolepis, about 2 feet long.

Bothriolepis, about 10 inches long.

Lunaspis, about 8 inches long.

Gorgonichthys jaw bones

Gorgonichthys, about 15 feet long.

Placoderms (Class Placodermi)
The **placoderms** or "plated skins" were heavily armored in overlapping large and small plates of bone that covered the head and trunk. In some forms, the jaws were equipped with pointed and shearing plates that functioned like teeth. Most had broad-based paired pectoral and pelvic fins resembling those of sharks.

Placoderms flourished until their extinction about 355 million years ago.

Dunkleosteus, about 20 feet long.

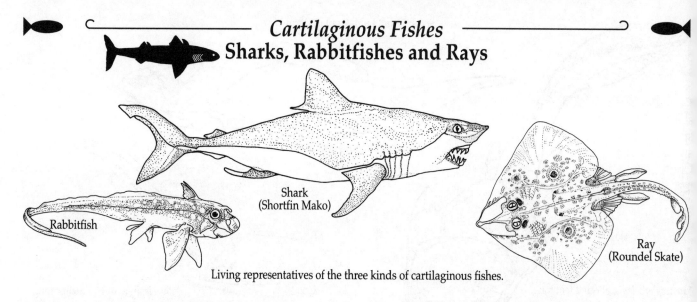

Living representatives of the three kinds of cartilaginous fishes.

The cartilaginous fishes (Class Chondrichthyes) include the sharks, rabbitfishes and rays, about 900 species world-wide.

Sharks have remained essentially unchanged since about 350 million years ago when we find the first complete shark fossils. However, fragmentary shark scales and teeth go back as far as 400 million years ago.

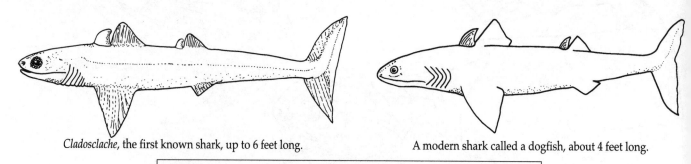

Cladosclache, the first known shark, up to 6 feet long.

A modern shark called a dogfish, about 4 feet long.

> Sharks have remained essentially unchanged since about 350 million years ago.

The Chondrichthyes do not have an internal skeleton of bone. Instead, their braincase, upper and lower jaws, gill arches, vertebrae and fin supports consist of a special kind of cartilage hardened with lime. The cartilaginous skeleton of sharks and their relatives was once considered "primitive" or "archaic". But now scientists consider this skeleton to be a specialization of benefit to the shark lifestyle. Chondrichthyes, unlike bony fishes (see page 26) do not have an air-bladder for providing buoyancy in the water. Instead, their light cartilaginous frame, coupled with a large oil-filled liver, serve to buoy them up. In addition, sharks have broad-based pectoral fins that provide lift in the water as long as they keep moving.

The upper and lower jaw cartilages of sharks are lined with rows of teeth. These grow throughout life from within the inner surface of the jaws and replace worn and damaged teeth in the front rows.

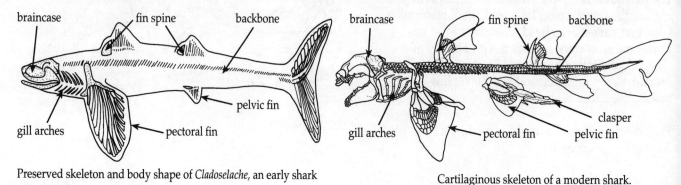

Preserved skeleton and body shape of *Cladoselache*, an early shark

Cartilaginous skeleton of a modern shark.

Unlike most other fishes, fertilization is internal in Chondrichthyes. The males have special structures called "claspers" attached to their pelvic fins. The claspers are folded together during mating to conduct sperm into the genital opening of the female.

Rabbitfishes, also called chimaeras (ki-mee-rahs), are an offshoot from sharks from about 340 million years ago. There are some 34 surviving species. These are mostly marine deep-water forms. They have a swollen-looking head, tapering back into a whip-like tail. Unlike other Chondrichthyes, they have a gill cover over their gill slits.

Female

Male

male claspers

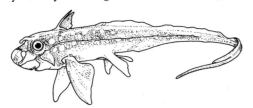

Modern rabbitfish, about 3 feet long.

Reconstruction of a pair of *Echinochimaera* — 100 million-year-old rabbitfishes.

Rays are another shark offshoot. The first fossil rays date from about 200 million years ago. Rays can be looked on as flattened sharks with large pectoral fins and reduced, whip-like tails. (The tail is often armed with a poisonous spine.) Rays swim entirely by wave-like motions of their wing-like pectorals. Their mouth faces downward and so do their gill slits. Some rays are surface-swimming filter-feeders, others crush shellfish and crustaceans on the bottom.

Some rays are called **skates**. These are generally bottom feeders. Unlike other rays which give birth to 2 to 8 live young, skates lay eggs. Each egg is encased in a horny container often found on beaches.

Skate egg capsule

Atlantic Stingray (*Dasyatis sabina*), up to 6 feet long.

Finetooth Shark (*Carcharhinus isodon*), up to 6 feet long.

Smalltooth Sawfish (*Pristis pectinosa*), up to 20 feet long.

Bull Shark (*Carcharhinus leucas*), up to 12 feet long.

All cartilaginous fishes are essentially marine species, and we will not consider any of them in our general overview of Texas' freshwater fishes later on in this book. However, some sharks and rays are coastal, living along shores and bays. Sometimes these wander up into rivers and streams. Texas has two sharks and two rays, the young of which can be found in estuaries and the lower reaches of rivers and streams. These are:

The Finetooth Shark (*Carcharhinus isodon*)
The Bull Shark (*Carcharhinus leucas*)
The Smalltooth Sawfish (*Pristis pectinosa*)
The Atlantic Stingray (*Dasyatis sabina*)

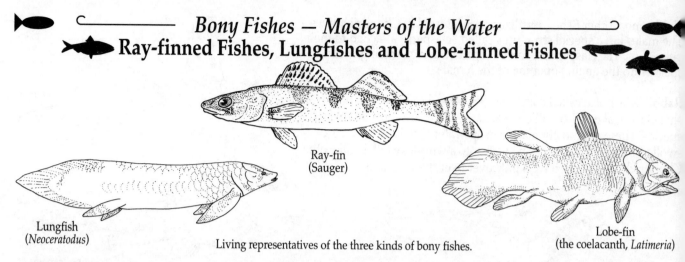

Ray-fin
(Sauger)

Lungfish
(*Neoceratodus*)

Lobe-fin
(the coelacanth, *Latimeria*)

Living representatives of the three kinds of bony fishes.

Today, the bony fishes (Class Osteichthyes) form the largest and most diverse group of backboned animals, containing some 25,000 species. The vast majority of bony fishes is represented by the **ray-finned fishes**, the **Actinopterygia** (act-ee-nop-ter-eagia), often called "actinopts" for short. Other once important but today almost extinct groups of bony fishes are the **lungfishes** (three living species) and the **lobe-finned fishes** (one living species).

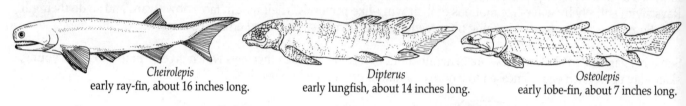

Cheirolepis
early ray-fin, about 16 inches long.

Dipterus
early lungfish, about 14 inches long.

Osteolepis
early lobe-fin, about 7 inches long.

Early representativies of the three kinds of bony fishes.

The earliest well-formed bony fish fossils date from almost 400 million years ago. All three groups of bony fishes were represented by that time.

All bony fishes have the following features in common:

1)   A **skeleton of bone** consisting of a skull (made of separate roof and cheek bones surrounding a solid braincase), gill arches, a vertebral column with attached ribs, shoulder and hip girdles, and fin supports. [Some of the earliest forms had partly cartilaginous skeletons.]

Fin supports in ray-fins are different from those of lobe-fins and lungfishes. Lungfishes and lobe-fins share a similar anatomy when it comes to the construction of their paired fins. In both groups the upper and central portions of these fins are "fleshy". That is because the fin supports consist of sturdy bony elements from which radiate the much thinner fin rays. In ray-fins, the paired fins are supported only by parallel fin rays and lack the heavier central elements. Ray-fins therefore do not have "fleshy" fins.

The arrangement of the bones in the skull is also quite different among the three groups of bony fishes.

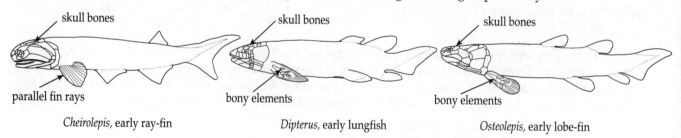

skull bones

parallel fin rays

skull bones

bony elements

skull bones

bony elements

Cheirolepis, early ray-fin

Dipterus, early lungfish

Osteolepis, early lobe-fin

Fin supports and skull bone arrangements in ray-fins are different from those of lobe-fins and lungfishes.

2)   **Lungs** (in early ray-fins and lungfishes) or an air-bladder (in all later ray-fins). Lungs were used for supplemental air gulping while the air-bladder of later forms became an organ for regulating buoyancy in the water.

lung
of primitive ray-fins

3)   A covering of interlocking **bony scales**. These were thick and heavy in early forms, but become thinner in later descendants.

air-bladder
of most modern ray-fins

Review: Name the scales.
(Hint: see page 6.)

_____ _____ _____

Lungfishes
Dipnoi (dip-noy)

African lungfish (*Protopterus*), about 1.5 feet long.

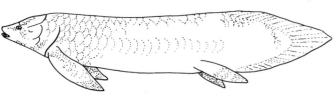

Australian lungfish (*Neoceratodus*), about 2 feet long.

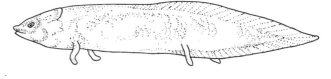

South American lungfish (*Lepidosiren*), about 1.5 feet long.

There are only three kinds of living **lungfishes,** also called Dipnoi. All of these supplement gill breathing with gulping air into their lungs (the Australian lungfish has only a single lung).

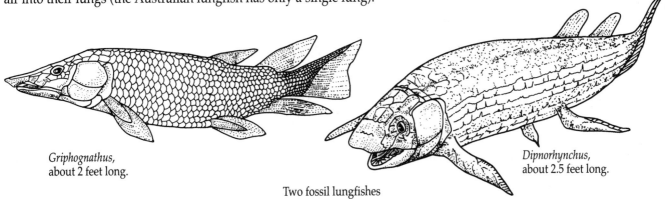

Griphognathus,
about 2 feet long.

Dipnorhynchus,
about 2.5 feet long.

Two fossil lungfishes

Lungfishes were quite successful as a group until about 250 million years ago when they began to decline in numbers. Fossils in burrows have been found showing that ancient lungfishes could lie dormant enclosed in baked mud during droughts just like the South American and African lungfishes do today.

Lobe-fins
Crossopterygia, (cross-op-ter-igia)

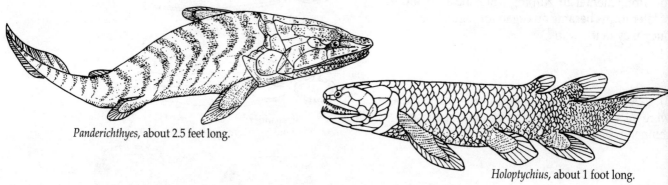

Panderichthyes, about 2.5 feet long.

Holoptychius, about 1 foot long.

Two extinct lobe-fins

The lobe-fins were a major group of fierce aquatic predators. Their main significance to us is that , about 375 million years ago, some of them gave rise to the first four-legged land-going vertebrates, the amphibians.

Today, only one species of lobe-fin (*Latimeria chalumnae*) survives in the seas around south-east Africa. It is the last member of a specialized marine group of lobe-fins called coelacanths.

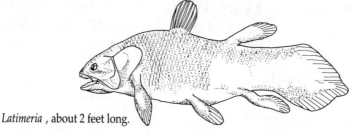

Latimeria , about 2 feet long.

One group of lobe-fins includes the ancestors of the amphibians. Certain of these lobe-fins moved onto the land where over millions of years their paired limbs were converted to weight-bearing front and hind limbs with digits. [Some of these early amphibians had up to 8 digits on the front and hind leg.]

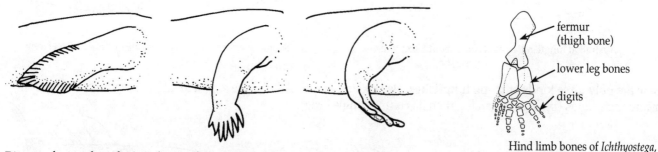

Diagram showing how the front (pectoral) fin developed into a front leg with digits.

fermur (thigh bone)

lower leg bones

digits

Hind limb bones of *Ichthyostega*, an early amphibian

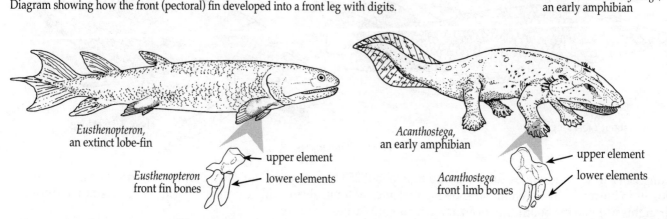

Eusthenopteron, an extinct lobe-fin

Eusthenopteron front fin bones

upper element

lower elements

Acanthostega, an early amphibian

Acanthostega front limb bones

upper element

lower elements

Ray-finned Bony Fishes
Actinopterygia (act-ee-nopt-er-igia)

The ray-fins (or "actinopts") are the dominant group of living fishes, numbering some 23,000 species. The earliest fossil ray-fins date from almost 400 million years ago. The group has been flourishing ever since, with their biggest spurt occurring from the age of dinosaurs onwards. (Ray-fins, surprisingly, were not affected by the mass extinctions 65 million years ago when the terrestrial dinosaurs as well as many marine groups died out.)

From their earliest beginnings, ray-fins can be distinguished from the other bony fishes by their not having paired fins with fleshy lobes. Instead, ray-fins have only parallel fin rays for fin support. Also, their skull bones are arranged differently. And, instead of the two dorsal fins of lungfishes and lobe-fins, ray-fins have a single dorsal fin. (This fin is sometimes divided into two in some modern forms.)

Ray-fin evolution can be divided into three phases. Fishes belonging to the earliest phase are called **chondrosteans** (con-dross-tee-ans), then come the "in between" **holosteans** (whole-oss-tee-ans) and finally, the **teleosteans** (teal-ee-oss-tee-ans) or the teleosts. Just about all the living marine and freshwater fishes are teleosts.

Unlike the primitive chondrosteans and the in-between holosteans, the advanced teleosts tend to have:

1) a homocercal (symmetrical) rather than a heterocercal tail (see page 14).
2) paired fins placed relatively far forward on the body (see page 5).
3) a buoyant air-bladder rather than lungs (see page 8).
4) a mouth that can be quickly levered open to suck in prey (see page 15).

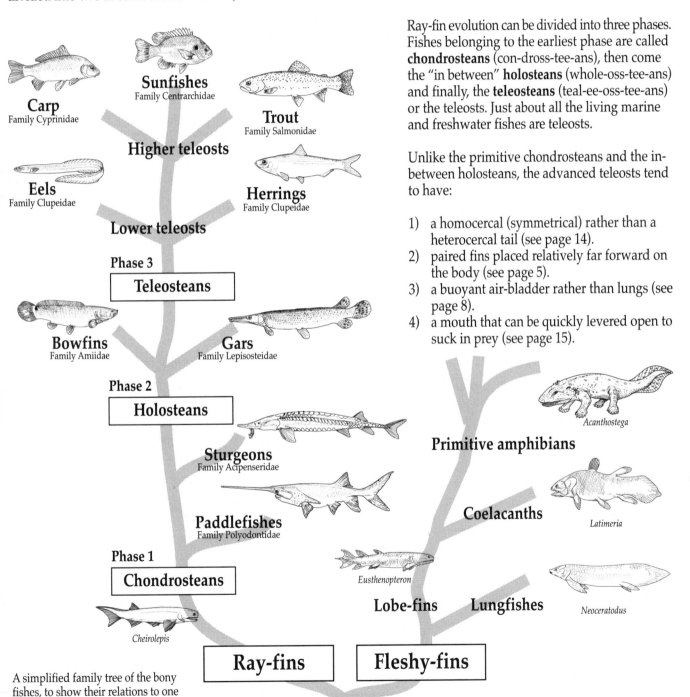

Carp
Family Cyprinidae

Sunfishes
Family Centrarchidae

Trout
Family Salmonidae

Higher teleosts

Eels
Family Clupeidae

Herrings
Family Clupeidae

Lower teleosts

Phase 3
Teleosteans

Bowfins
Family Amiidae

Gars
Family Lepisosteidae

Phase 2
Holosteans

Acanthostega

Primitive amphibians

Sturgeons
Family Acipenseridae

Latimeria

Coelacanths

Paddlefishes
Family Polyodontidae

Phase 1
Chondrosteans

Eusthenopteron

Neoceratodus

Lobe-fins   **Lungfishes**

Cheirolepis

Ray-fins   **Fleshy-fins**

A simplified family tree of the bony fishes, to show their relations to one another and to the amphibians.

Lampreys — Family Petromyzontidae

Lampreys are considered a surviving offshoot from ancient jawless armored fishes called ostracoderms (see page 20). Adult lampreys are eel-like in appearance. They are scaleless, have a cartilaginous skeleton, a single nostril on the top of the head, several pairs of port-like gill openings and two dorsal fins continuous with the tail fin. The jawless mouth consists of a rounded cup, lined with rasping teeth. They are usually parasitic as adults. Spawning takes place in nests excavated on the bottom of streams. The eggs (anywhere from 1,000 to 10,000 depending on the species) hatch into blind larvae called **ammocoetes**. These worm-like larvae burrow into muddy-bottomed pools where they remain from 3 to 8 years, filtering micro-organisms through their pharynx and gill openings. This is much in the manner of the lancelet, *Amphioxus*, considered to be representative of ancestral vertebrates (see page 19). In most species, after the change-over from larva to adult, the adults migrate to larger streams, lakes or the ocean. There they attach themselves to a fish host with their suckerlike mouths and, by rasping a hole in its side, suck out its fluids and tissues. Often the host fish actually survives such an attack. The adults of what are called brook lampreys are nonparasitic. After metamorphosis, they do not feed, and spawn the following spring. Brook lampreys' oral disc teeth are small and reduced in number and the intestine is either absent or only weakly developed.

A total of 38 species of lampreys are known from North America and Eurasia. Of these, 19 inhabit North America north of Mexico, with Texas having 2 species (one parasitic and one nonparasitic).

ammocoete

Chestnut Lamprey — *Ichthyomyzon castaneus*
Large mouth disc wider than head; yellow or tan above, lighter below; olive-yellow fins; black lateral line organs. Adults have well developed intestine. Parasitic. To 18 inches. Range in Texas: eastern Texas lakes and streams of the Red, Sabine and Neches basins.

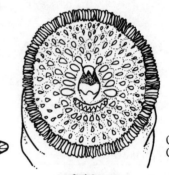

Oral disc of a
Chestnut Lamprey

Southern Brook Lamprey — *Ichthyomyzon gagei*
Mouth disc narrower than head; gray or tan above, lighter below; yellowish fins; black lateral line organs. Intestine not developed in adults. Nonparasitic. To 6.5 inches. Range in Texas: eastern Texas creeks and small rivers of the Red, Sabine and Neches basins.

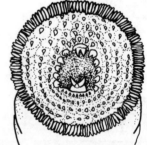

Oral disc of a
Southern Brook
Lamprey

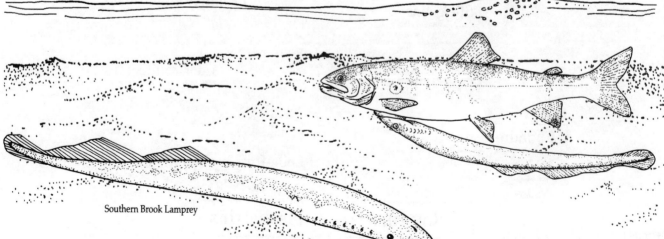

Southern Brook Lamprey

Sturgeons — Family Acipenseridae

Sturgeons are "living fossils". They are thought to be surviving chondrosteans, the earliest ray-finned bony fishes to appear in the fossil record (see page 29). Sturgeons have a cartilaginous skeleton (while their fossil ancestors had a partly bony skeleton) and a heterocercal tail (see page 14) that is, one in which the backbone extends into a longer upper lobe. All sturgeons are large, enter freshwater at least to spawn, but some species are mostly marine. Distinguishing features are a strong, round body, a pointed snout with large fleshy barbels, a mouth surrounded by fleshy "lips" located on the underside, and large bony plates on the head and in rows along the back and sides. Sturgeons are commercially important for their flesh as well as their eggs (called caviar). Populations of sturgeons have been badly reduced worldwide due to overfishing and the bad effects of dams and pollution. Sturgeons are "benthic cruisers", moving along the bottom and stirring up invertebrates which they suck up with their mouths. Older sturgeons also feed on fish.

There are 23 species in Europe, Asia and North America, of which Texas has one.

Shovelnose Sturgeon — *Scaphirhynchus platorynchus*
The most southern of the North American sturgeons. It has a flat shovelnosed snout with four fringed barbels on the underside. Light brown or buff above, white below; bony scutes surround the rear part of body; scale-like scutes on the belly. Hard, curved spines on the leading edge of the pectoral fins are used like legs to drag itself along the bottom. Frequents river channels and embayments. To 34 inches. Range in Texas: in the Red River below Lake Texoma.

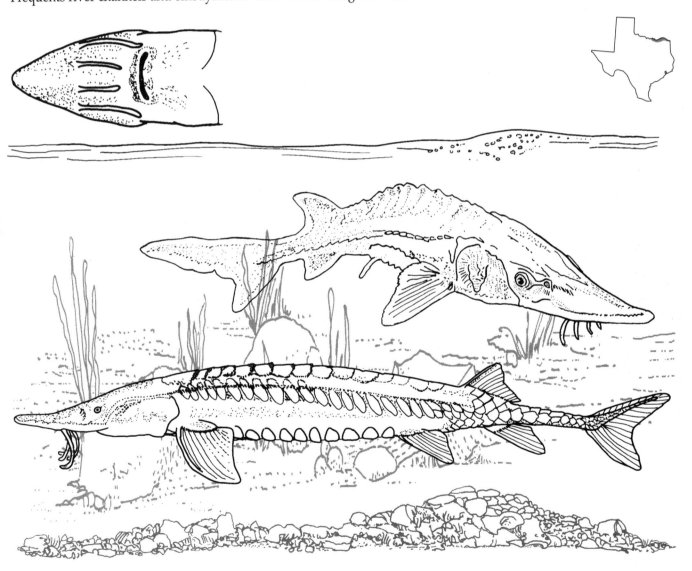

Paddlefishes — Family Polyodontidae

Like the sturgeons, the two species of paddlefishes are considered to be surviving chondrosteans (see page 29). They have a skeleton of cartilage, a heterocercal tail and a long, paddle-shaped snout. One species inhabits the Mississippi and adjacent Gulf Coast drainages of North America. This is the species found in Texas. The other species of paddlefish has a more sword-like beak and is China's largest (up to 21 feet) freshwater fish. The extended snouts of paddlefishes are covered with electric organs capable of detecting concentrations of prey.

Paddlefish — *Polyodon spathula*

Large unscaled fish with a snout shaped like a paddle. The snout is about one-third the body length. The mouth is huge and toothless. There is a fleshy pointed flap on the rear of the gill cover. The eyes are tiny. Gray to blue-gray, often mottled above; white below. Feeds on zooplankton (tiny floating and swimming animals) captured by swimming through the water with an open mouth and filtering out the plankton through the gills. Locally called "freshwater shark". Attains a length of 6 feet and weight of 150 pounds. Range in Texas: used to occur in every large river from Trinity basin eastward; since 1950, its numbers have been greatly reduced. **Endangered**.

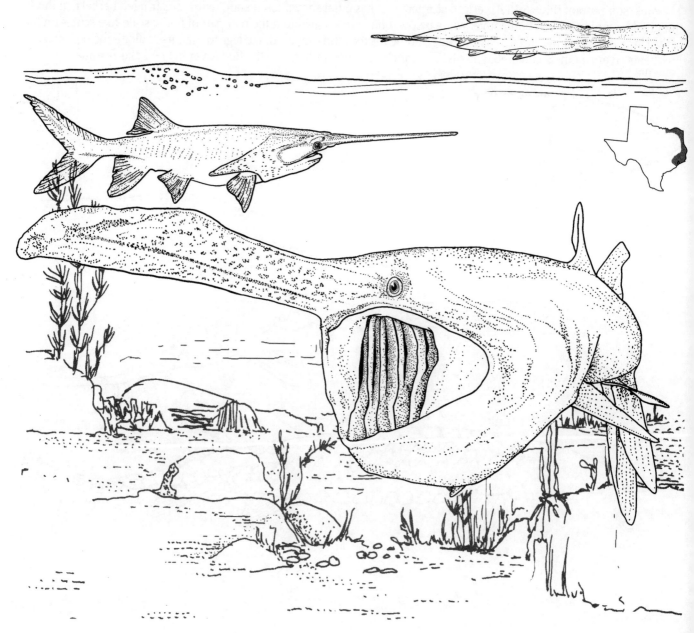

Gars — Family Lepisosteidae

The seven living species of gars are native to North America. They are primitive fishes considered to be surviving holosteans, an ancient bony fish group (see page 29). Their cylindrical bodies are covered with thick, diamond-shaped, non-overlapping ganoid scales. Their hard, bony heads have long snouts with sharp, conspicuous teeth. They have a rounded heterocercal tail. Their large air-bladders make them buoyant despite their heavy body armor. Their air-bladder also functions as a lung, especially when the waters they live in turn stagnant. Gars are mostly lie-in-wait predators, darting out after prey which they seize sideways, turn around and then swallow whole. However, they also frequently feed on sick, dying and dead fish. Gars lay their sticky eggs on aquatic plants. The developing young cling to the plant stems with an adhesive disc until ready to swim. Texas has four of the species found in the United States.

Alligator Gar — *Lepisosteus spatula*
A giant among gars, reaching almost 10 feet. The snout is short and broad with the upper jaw shorter than the rest of the head. Unlike all the other gar species, the upper jaw has two rows of teeth. Dark olive-brown (sometimes black) above, occasionally spotted; white to yellow below. Inhabits sluggish pools and backwaters of large rivers, swamps and bayous. Range in Texas: coastal rivers and streams from the Red River to the Rio Grande.

Longnose Gar — *Lepisosteus osseus*
Long narrow snout, twice as long as the rest of the head. Olive-brown above, white below; dark spots on the median fins. To 72 inches. Inhabits sluggish pools, back waters and oxbows of medium to large rivers and lakes. Range in Texas: most rivers.

Alligator Gar

Longnose Gar

Shortnose Gar — *Lepisosteus platostomus*

Relatively short, broad snout (but not quite as short as the alligator gar's). Olive or brown above, white below; black spots usually only on the dorsal fins. Found in quiet pools and backwaters of creeks and small rivers, swamps and lakes often near submerged vegetation. To 33 inches. Range in Texas: only the Red River drainage below Lake Texoma.

Spotted Gar — *Lepisosteus oculatus*

Medium long snout. Many olive-brown to black spots on the body, head and all of the fins. Olive-brown to black above; white to yellow below. To 44 inches. Lives in quiet clear pools and backwaters of lowland creeks, rivers, oxbow lakes and bayous. Range in Texas: coastal streams from the Red River to the Guadalupe River.

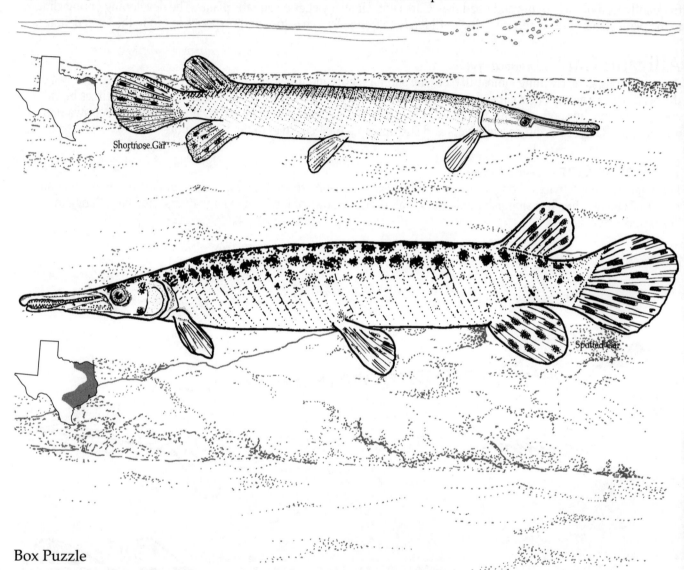

Box Puzzle

Each of the letter boxes throughout the book contains an 8-letter word. It can be found by starting at one of the letters and reading either **clockwise** or **counter-clockwise**. In the example below the word REDHORSE is found by starting at the **R** in the lower left corner and reading clockwise.

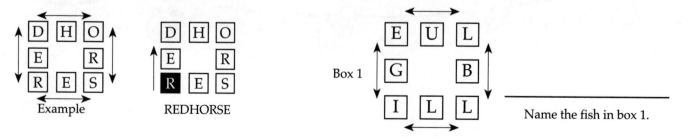

Name the fish in box 1.

Bowfins — Family Amiidae

This ancient, once world-wide family has one living representative: the bowfin, *Amia calva*, of North America. Considered a surviving holostean (see page 29), the bowfin retains a rounded heterocercal tail and lunglike air-bladder.

Bowfin — *Amia calva*

Long, nearly cylindrical body, large head. Cycloid scales. The long dorsal fin runs along more than half of the back. The nostrils are tubular. The large mouth has many teeth and extends behind the eye. The underside of the head has a large bony plate. Mottled olive above; cream yellow to pale green below. Black bands on the dorsal and tail fins. Prominent black spot near the upper base of the tail fin. (In young and male bowfins this spot is surrounded by an orange ring.) Bowfins can breathe air with their lunglike air-bladders, especially during droughts when they survive by lying torpid in muddy pools. Spawning occurs in the spring in circular nests made by the male who also guards the nest and, for a while, the newly hatched young. Inhabits swamps, sloughs and backwaters of lowland streams. To 43 inches. Range in Texas: in the Red, San Jacinto and Sabine River systems and downstream reaches of the Brazos and Colorado basins.

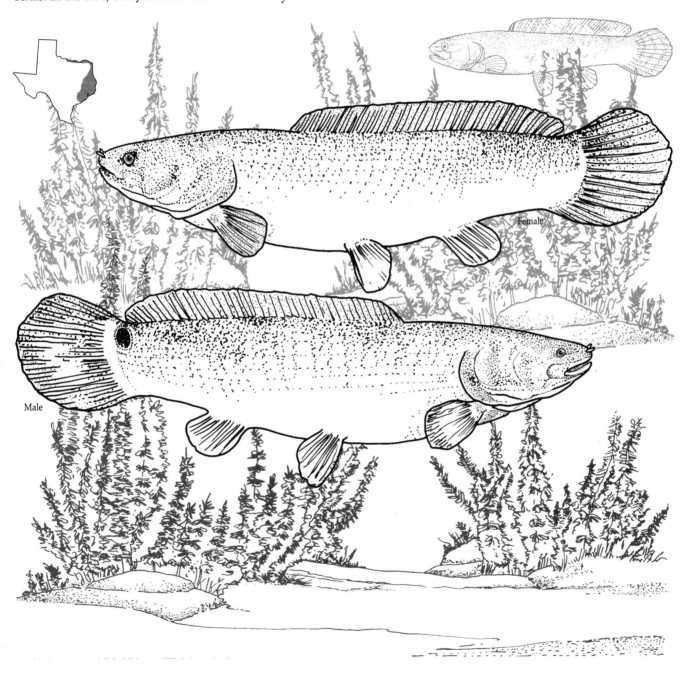

Female

Male

Freshwater Eels — Family Anguillidae

This teleost family of 15 species is known from every continent except Antarctica. Freshwater eels are snakelike in shape and have a small ridged mouth that cannot be pushed forward in the manner of most teleosts (see page 29). They do not have pelvic fins and their elongated dorsal and anal fins are continuous with the tail fin. Scales are either absent or so small as to be hardly noticeable. The gill openings are placed far back and covered by a flexible gill cover. The two best known representatives of this family are the American Eel (*Anguilla rostrata*) and the closely related European Eel (*Anguilla anguilla*). Both species (as do most eels) undergo long migrations when they are ready to reproduce (see below).

[Starting with eels, all the fishes discussed from this point are teleosts.]

American Eel — *Anguilla rostrata*
Slender snakelike body; no visible scales; small pointed head, with lower jaw projecting well beyond the upper jaw. Yellow to olive-brown above; pale yellow to white below. To 60 inches. When they are ready to reproduce, these eels migrate from fresh water to a place in the Atlantic Ocean south of Bermuda called the Sargasso Sea. After spawning at great depths, the adult eels die. From the eggs hatch thin transparent larvae called **leptocephalus** (meaning "leaf-like") **larvae** that migrate back to the shores of North America and South America. The larvae take about a year to reach American coasts. There they transform into **elvers** (small, miniature eels) and move up streams and estuaries. Males remain in brackish water in streams along the coast. Females usually move far upstream and remain there from 6 to 12 years. When ready to spawn, adult eels change to a silvery color and migrate out to sea, using deepwater currents to carry them to the Sargasso Sea (see page 1). During their freshwater existence, eels generally hide out in crevices and among vegetation from where they hunt other fishes. Range in Texas: in all major river systems in East Texas below the dams that now prevent movement into Central and Western Texas.

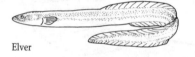

Elver

leptocephalus larva

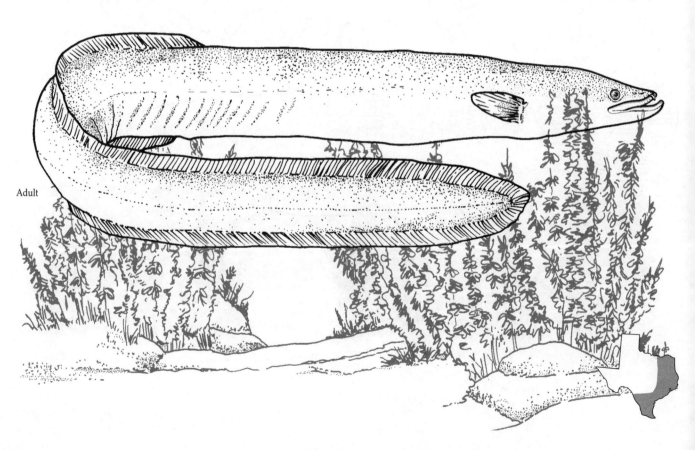

Adult

Herrings and Shads — Family Clupeidae

This family includes herrings, shads, sardines, menhaden and others (about 180 species). Members of this family — the clupeids— tend to congregate in well-lit waters where they school and feed on plankton (both plant and animal). Although mainly marine, quite a few (for example, gizzard shad) are abundant in fresh water, especially lakes and reservoirs, while still others (for example, shad) migrate into fresh water to spawn. Family characteristics include: silvery scales; a compressed body form; a "sawtooth" belly formed by a row of keeled scales along the underside; no lateral line; no scales on the head; an upturned mouth (for plankton gathering). Clupeids also have excellent underwater hearing due to an extension of their air-bladder that connects to the inner ear. Texas has three species of clupeids.

Skipjack Herring— *Alosa chrysochloris*
Strongly oblique jaws; blue-green above sharply separated from silvery sides and bottom. To 21 inches. Inhabits medium to large rivers and reservoirs. A schooling species found in flowing water over sandy bottoms. Like the gizzard shad (see below) can be observed leaping out of the water or skipping along the surface on its side. Range in Texas: coastal streams of eastern Texas; also in Gulf waters.

Gizzard Shad — *Dorosoma cepedianum*
Long whiplike last dorsal fin ray; blunt snout; upper jaw overhangs lower jaw; deep notch at center of upper jaw. Purple-blue spot near upper edge of the gill cover — faint or absent in large adults. Silver-blue above grading to silver-white on sides; no black specks on chin or floor of mouth. To 20.5 inches. Found in deep, open water in medium to large rivers, lakes and reservoirs. Often enters brackish water. Range in Texas: all major streams and reservoirs; often constitutes more than half of the total weight of fish in a given body of water.

Threadfin Shad — *Dorosoma petenense*
Similar to gizzard shad but has more pointed snout, no overhanging upper jaw and spots are present on chin and floor of mouth. The fins are yellowish and the purple shoulder spot persists in large adults. Usually found on upper waters with no noticeable current in lakes, backwaters and pools of medium and large rivers. To 9 inches. Range in Texas: common in all eastern Texas streams; introduced as a forage fish (food for other game fishes) in reservoirs all over the state.

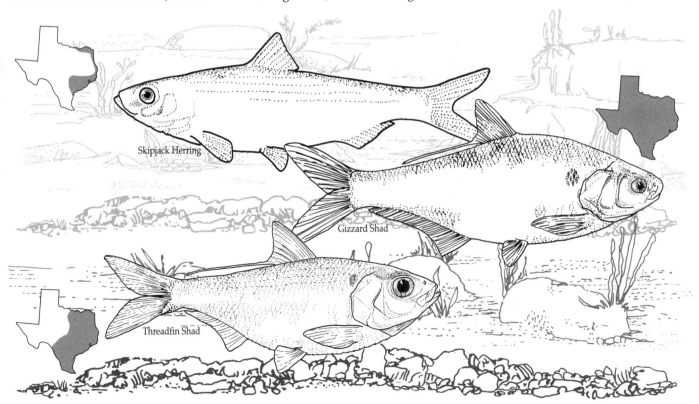

Skipjack Herring

Gizzard Shad

Threadfin Shad

Mooneyes — Family Hiodontidae

This North American family has two species, only one of which, the Goldeye (see below), is officially reported from Texas. (The other, called the Mooneye, is thought to occur in the north-east corner of Texas.) They resemble members of the herring family (see page 37), but have a lateral line and an untoothed, smooth keel along the belly. Their silvery bodies are strongly compressed (flattened from side to side) and they have no scales on the head. Their eggs, unlike other North American freshwater fishes, are buoyant and drift downstream after spawning.

Goldeye — *Hiodon alosoides*
Deep compressed body; fleshy keel along belly extends from pectoral fin to anal fin. Blue-greenish above, silvery-white on sides and below; large mouth; blunt round snout. Golden eye color is due to a special structure inside the eye that gives them good night vision. To 20 inches. Occurs in deep, open pools and channels of large, lowland rivers, lakes and reservoirs where they feed on aquatic insects and small fishes. Range in Texas: only in Red River basin; especially abundant in Lake Texoma.

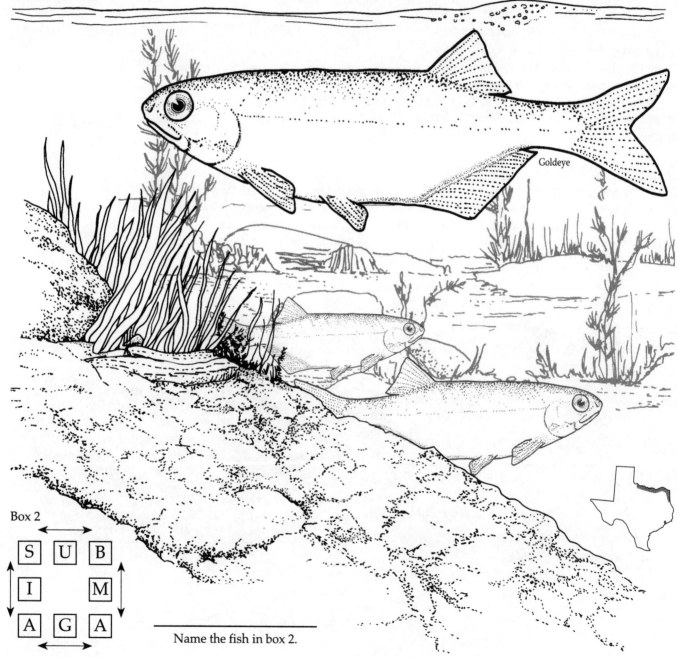

Goldeye

Box 2

S	U	B
I		M
A	G	A

Name the fish in box 2.

Trouts, Salmons, Chars and Whitefishes — Family Salmonidae

Only one member, the rainbow trout (see below), of this mainly cold-water family of about 70 species can be found in Texas. And, this species is not native, but introduced. Another species of salmonid, the cutthroat trout, was probably once native to creeks in the Guadalupe and Davis mountains of Trans-Pecos Texas. It is now extinct in the state. All salmonids are either freshwater or migrate into freshwater to spawn after spending time in the ocean. Salmonids have sleek, streamlined bodies covered in tiny cycloid scales. In addition to a single dorsal fin, they have a small fleshy fin, called an adipose fin, located farther down along the back.

Rainbow Trout — *Oncorhynchus mykiss*

Graceful, streamlined shape; slightly forked tail. Back is usually dark-olive, shading to silvery white on underside. The body along with the tail fin is heavily speckled and has a pinkish stripe running along each side. To 42 inches. Rainbow trout are a cool-to-cold-water species native to the Pacific slope of North America from Alaska into Mexico. When in coastal streams, juveniles migrate into the ocean and return as adults to spawn. ["Sea-run" rainbow trout are called steelheads.] Eggs are laid in shallow nests dug out by the female. Rainbow trout eat insects, small crustaceans, snails and fish. Range in Texas: widely introduced in the state to provide winter-time fishing sport; however, in Texas high temperatures prevent reproductive or even summer survival of the stocked fish in most areas; successful spawning has been reported only from McKittrick Canyon in the Guadalupe Mountains.

Rainbow trout

Pikes and Pickerels — Family Esocidae

Members of this family are long, sleek, predatory fishes with a large, fixed mouth lined with sharp teeth. They are lie-in-wait hunters that prey on other fish. The snout is duckbill-like. Dorsal and anal fins are located far back on the body. Esocids are mostly north-temperate species native to Eurasia and North America. Of the approximately 10 species in this family, three occur in Texas. One, the Northern Pike, *Esox lucius*, has been introduced to several northern reservoirs in the state, while the other two, the Grass Pickerel and the Chain Pickerel (see below) are native to east Texas.

Chain Pickerel — *Esox niger*
Green chainlike pattern on yellow side (adult), wave lines on young. The strong black bar below the eye is vertical. To 39 inches. Found in vegetated lakes, swamps and backwaters of creeks and small to medium rivers. Range in Texas: eastern Texas drainages of the Red and Sabine basins.

Grass Pickerel — *Esox americanus*
Dark olive above, numerous dark green to brown wavy bars along side of adult; amber to white below; yellow green fins; long narrow dished-in (concave) snout. Black bar below eye slants toward rear. To 15 inches. Frequents lakes, swamps and sluggish pools of streams. Range in Texas: eastern Texas from Red River basin south to the Brazos River basin.

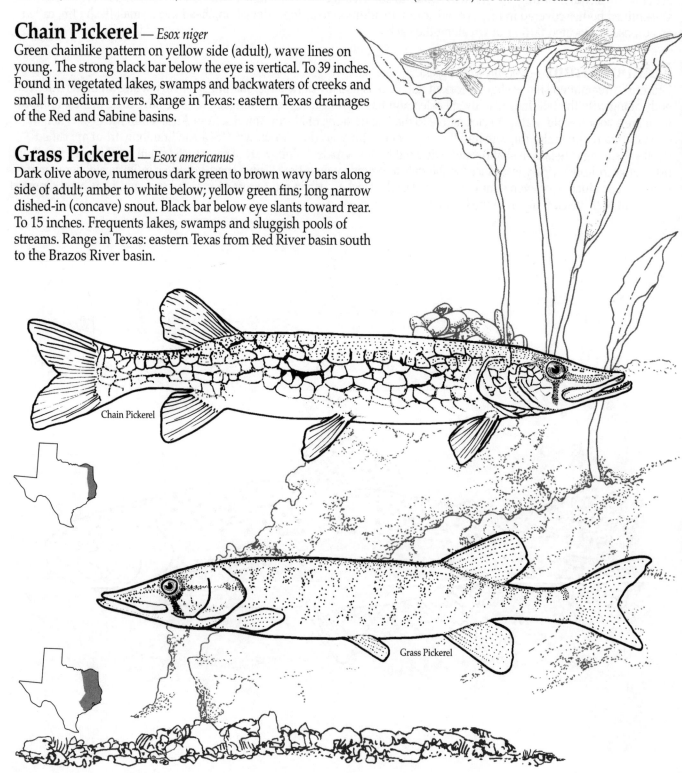

Chain Pickerel

Grass Pickerel

Characins — Family Characidae

This huge family of about 800, mostly small fishes is found mainly in Central America, South America and Africa. Characins are closely related to minnows (see page 42), but unlike minnows, characins have an adipose fin (a small fleshy fin behind the dorsal fin) and teeth on the jaws. Many are brightly colored and popular aquarium fishes. Only one species is native to North America. This is the Mexican Tetra of southern Texas.

Mexican Tetra — *Astyanax mexicanus*
Mostly silvery, deeply compressed body, blunt snout; large sharp teeth in terminal mouth; adipose fin. Black horizontal stripe on tail fin and caudal peduncle (the narrow portion of the body in front of the tail fin). Large adults have yellow fins with red markings on the tail, anal and pelvic fins. To 4.75 inches. Range in Texas: native to Nueces River, lower Rio Grande and lower Pecos drainages; now established through introduction by "bait bucket" release in streams of the Edwards Plateau (and also in New Mexico Pecos River drainages).

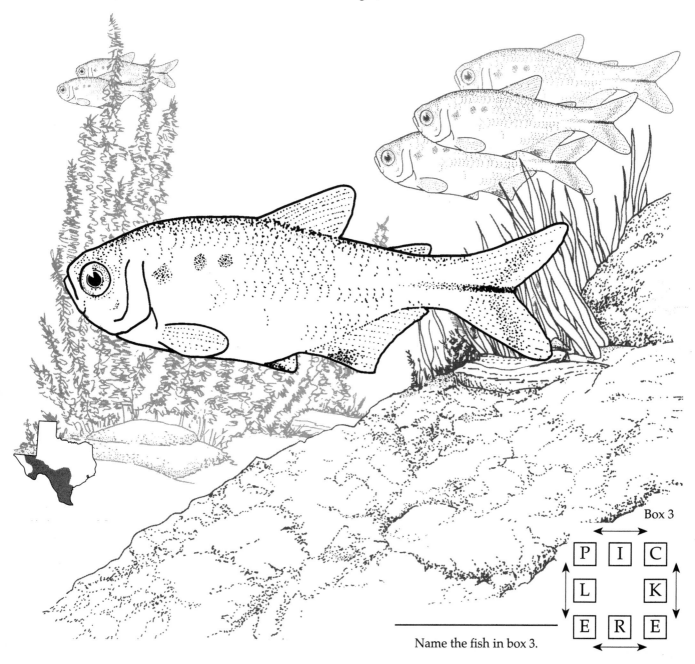

Box 3

P	I	C
L		K
E	R	E

_____

Name the fish in box 3.

Minnows — Family Cyprinidae

Although the term "minnow" is often used for any small fish, only members of the family Cyprinidae — the cyprinids — should technically be called minnows. Cyprinids include a large variety of fishes, some relatively large, like the carp, but most of small to medium size. Common names for various cyprinids include the terms "minnow", "shiner", "chub", "dace" and "stoneroller". The best known cyprinids are probably the goldfish and the carp, both native to Asia but now introduced all over the world.

There are some 2,100 species of cyprinids native to North America, Eurasia and Africa. North America has 231 species, of which Texas has 56.

Family characteristics include: a "classic" fish shape with a single dorsal fin; the pelvic fins located on the underside near the middle of the body; a lateral line (there are a few exceptions); and cycloid scales. There are no true spines in the fins, although carp and goldfish have a few hardened fin rays. The mouth is small and toothless, but there are from one to three rows of teeth, called **pharyngeal teeth**, located along the lower half of the last gill arch (see page 15). These teeth work against a horny pad on the base of the skull.

Minnows are very diverse ecologically. Members of the two large genera, *Notropis* and *Cyprinella*, which are usually called "shiners", are mostly carnivorous, feeding on small crustaceans and insects. Plant-eating cyprinids include the algae-scraping "stonerollers" and some of the "silvery minnows". These plant-eaters, unlike the carnivores, have long coiled intestines which can be seen through the body wall.

Minnows have many different spawning habits. The males of some species build mounds of stones into which the eggs are laid. Others make nests under stones, and still others cement their eggs to vegetation. Breeding males often sport bright colors and "nuptial" tubercles which are shed after the spawning season.

Common Carp — *Cyprinus carpio*
Heavy-bodied with two barbels, rear one much larger, on each the side of upper jaw. Brassy green or yellow to golden brown or silvery above, yellow-white below. Long dorsal fin. Dorsal and anal fin have a heavy spine up front. Originally, native to Asia. Feed on both plant and animal material. To 48 inches. Some individuals have just a few enlarged scales and are known as "mirror carp". Some are scaleless and called "leather carp". Range in Texas: statewide, especially in large bodies of water.

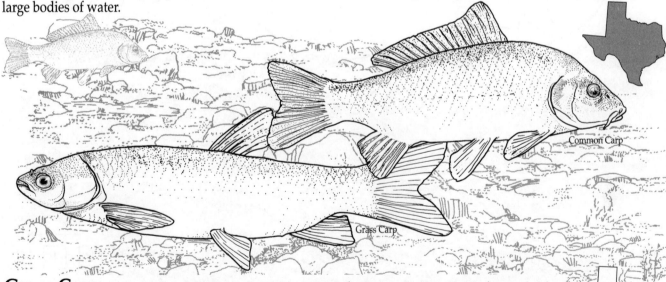

Common Carp

Grass Carp

Grass Carp — *Ctenopharyngodon idella*   Wide scaleless head on cylindrical body (more slender than common carp). Narrow but high dorsal fin. Large, dark-edged scales. Gray to brassy-green above; white to yellow below. To 49 inches. Native to Asia; now introduced worldwide. Range in Texas: sterile grass carp are used widely for vegetation control in many private ponds and some public reservoirs; however, fertile grass carp are now reproducing in Trinity River-Galveston Bay area.

Central Stoneroller — *Campostoma anomalum*

Thick body; tan to brown above; often dark stripe along side. Hard ridge on lower jaw. Long coiled intestine visible through body wall. Breeding male has tubercles on head and nape, and orange dorsal and anal fins with a black band (made up of radiating lines). To 8.5 inches. Inhabits rocky riffles and pools of headwaters of streams and small rivers. Range in Texas: primarily in Central Texas on the Edwards Plateau, but also as far west as Devils River and north to Red River.

Blacktailed Shiner — *Cyprinella venusta*

Fairly deep body; pointed snout. Large black spot on base of tail fin. Dusky olive above; narrow black stripe along back; silvery sides. Breeding male has darker sides and yellowish to red-orange fins (except dorsal). To 7.5 inches. Common in sandy pools and runs of creeks and small rivers. Range in Texas: most streams in eastern Texas and on the Edwards Plateau.

Mississippi Silvery Minnow — *Hybognathus nuchalis*

Stout body, especially the front half; dorsal fin pointed. Light-brown to yellow olive above; dusky stripe along back; brilliant silver sides. The long coiled intestine is useful in digesting algae and other materials grubbed from the bottom. To 7 inches. Lives in pools and backwaters of slow flowing creeks and small rivers. Range in Texas: eastern Texas streams from Brazos River eastward and northward to Red River; also Pecos-Rio Grande drainages.

Central Stoneroller male

Blacktailed Shiner

Mississippi Silvery Minnow

Texas Shiner — *Notropis amabilis*

Sleek compressed body, with large eyes and black lips. Clear stripe above black stripe along silvery sides. To 2.5 inches. Inhabits rocky or sandy runs as well as pools of clear springs and streams. Typically found in schools. Hunts small crustaceans and insects. Range in Texas: in Edwards Plateau streams from the San Gabriel River to the Pecos River.

Ghost Shiner — *Notropis buchanani*

"Ghost-like" translucent milky white overall. (Sometimes scales along back may be faintly outlined, and black specks may occur on snout and along lateral line.) Compressed body arches toward dorsal fin then tapers sharply towards tail. Large pointed fins. To 2.5 inches. Found in quiet pools and backwaters, usually over sand, of rivers. Range in Texas: from Lower Rio Grande northward across middle of eastern Texas to the Red River.

Silverband Shiner — *Notropis shumardi*

Tall pointed dorsal fin. Compressed body. Light olive above; dusky stripe along back; silver stripe along side (often dusky at rear). To 4 inches. Inhabits pools and runs of large, often muddy rivers. Range in Texas: eastern Texas from Brazos River to Lavaca River drainage; also in lower Red River drainage.

Pallid Shiner — *Notropis (Hybopsis) amnis*

Body arched along the back (at beginning of the dorsal fin). Large, horizontally elliptical eye. Long snout overhanging subterminal mouth. Straw-yellow above, black stripe along silver side and around snout. Breeding male has tubercles mostly on lower half of head. To 3.25 inches. Inhabits sandy and silty pools of small to large rivers. Range in Texas: along Gulf Coastal Plain in eastern Texas to Guadalupe Basin.

Texas Shiner

Ghost Shiner

Silverband Shiner

Pallid Shiner

Blackspot Shiner — *Notropis atrocaudalis*

Narrow black stripe along side; black rectangular spot on base of caudal fin separate from stripe. Stocky body; small eye; subterminal mouth. Olive above; wide dusky stripe along back, silvery side. To 3 inches. Found in sandy and rocky runs and pools of creeks and small rivers, usually in shallow waters. Range in Texas: eastern Texas, from lower Brazos river basin north and east to Red River.

Bluehead Shiner — *Notropis (Pterunotropis) hubbsi*

Broad black stripe along side from chin, through eye, to caudal fin where it extends into spot. Breeding male has bright blue top of head; dorsal and caudal fins become huge. Dusky orange-brown above with dark stripe along back; stripe along side. To 2.5 inches. Found near vegetation in backwaters, oxbows and sluggish pools of creeks and small rivers. Range in Texas: only in Caddo Lake. **Threatened**.

Mimic Shiner — *Notropis volucellus*

Slender compressed body; broad rounded snout. Scales along side much deeper than wide. Gray to yellowish above, dusky stripe along silver side (stripe widest at rear). To 3 inches. Found in sandy pools of backwaters, creeks and rivers; also quiet lake waters. Range in Texas: eastern half of the state from Nueces basin northward, but not in Red River.

Chub Shiner — *Notropis potteri*

Wide, flattened head tapering to pronounced snout. Eye high on head. Dull olive to tan above; thin dusky stripe along back; scattered black spots along silver side merging into black streak towards rear. To 4.5 inches. Found in sandy runs of small to large rivers. Range in Texas: through most of Red River and Brazos River basins; also known from San Jacinto drainages near Conroe.

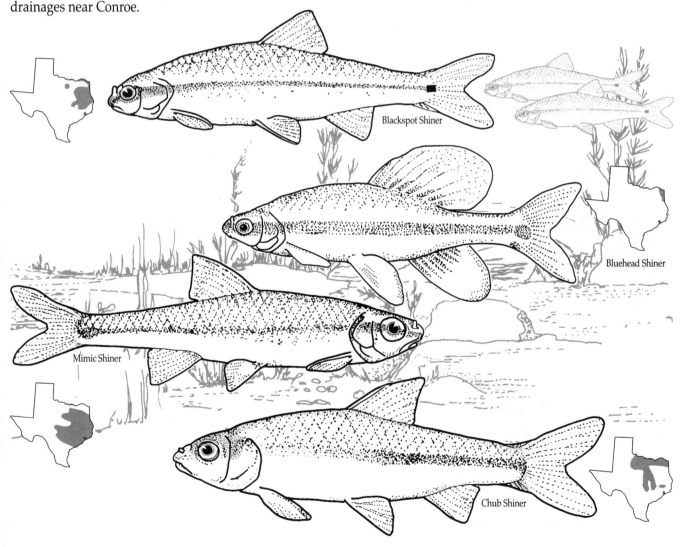

Blackspot Shiner

Bluehead Shiner

Mimic Shiner

Chub Shiner

Ribbon Shiner — *Lythrurus fumeus*

Slender, compressed body. Pale olive above; dusky stripe along back; silver-black stripe along side, darkest at rear. Speckled chin and lips. To 2.75 inches. Scales on neck outlined in black. Lives in quiet, muddy pools of headwaters and creeks. Range in Texas: Coastal Plains of eastern and northeastern Texas from Lavaca drainage north to Red River.

Speckled Chub — *Macrohybopsis (Extrarius) aestivalis*

Long slender body flattened below; bulbous snout overhangs mouth which has one or two barbels in each corner. Many small black spots on the back and side. Translucent; light olive to yellowish above; silvery sides often iridescent blue. To 3 inches. Lives in sand and gravel runs of streams and rivers. Range in Texas: throughout the state.

Pugnose Minnow — *Opsopoeodus emiliae*

Slender body; cross-hatched pattern on back and most of side; small, upturned mouth. Dusky olive above; dark stripe along silver side of head and body. Breeding male has bright white lower anal and pelvic fins. To 2.5 inches. Inhabits vegetated lakes, swamps, oxbows and sluggish streams. Range in Texas: streams of Coastal Plain in eastern Texas; also in Trinity River near Dallas.

Ribbon Shiner

Speckled Chub

Pugnose Minnow

Roundnose Minnow — *Dionda episcopa*

Black line along sides separates yellow-green above from silvery-white below. Dark green stripe along back. Yellow fins on adult. Compressed body; rounded snout with small subterminal mouth. Plant material in the long coiled gut often makes the belly look discolored. To 3 inches. Inhabits rocky pools of headwaters, creeks and small rivers. Range in Texas: headwaters of Edwards Plateau and West Texas streams of the Colorado, Guadalupe and Pecos drainages.

Bullhead Minnow — *Pimephales vigilax*

Slender body; square in cross-section; rounded snout. Large eye high on head. Large black spot at front of dorsal and tail fin. Olive above, scales clearly outlined; dusky stripe along silvery side. Breeding male has black head with silver bar behind head and large breeding tubercles on snout. To 3.5 inches. Inhabits quiet pools and runs over sand or gravel in medium rivers. Range in Texas: throughout the state; populations in upper Rio Grande basin and upper Red and Canadian basins have been introduced.

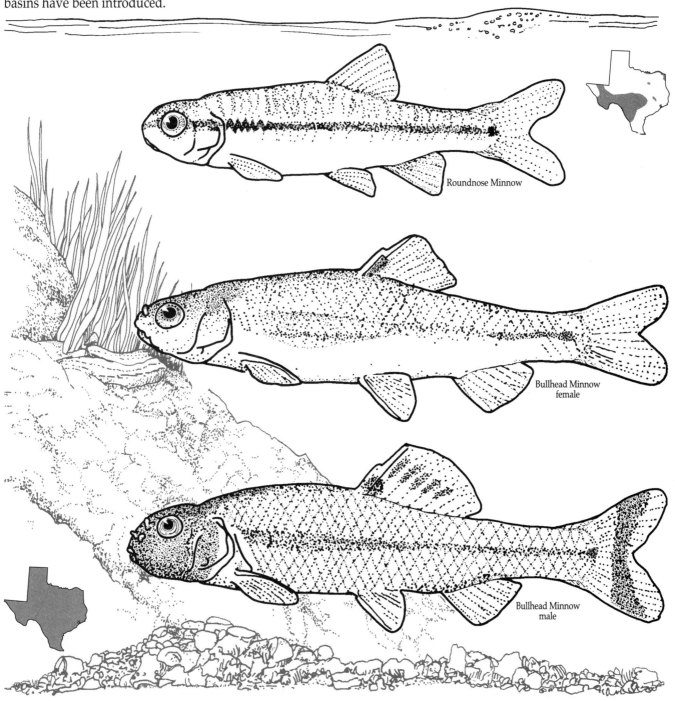

Roundnose Minnow

Bullhead Minnow
female

Bullhead Minnow
male

Creek Chub — *Semotilus atromaculatus*

Thick body; broad head with pointed snout. Small flaplike barbel in corner of large terminal mouth. Olive-brown above; dark stripe along back; dusky stripe along green-silver side and around snout; black bar in back of gill cover. Breeding male has pink lower half of body and yellow fins. To 12 inches. Found in rocky and sandy pools of headwaters of creeks and small rivers. Breeding males dig a series of pits in gravel along the bottom. Spawning takes place over the pits. Males guard the eggs and developing young. Range in Texas: smaller streams of eastern Texas and coastal waters of Brazos River Basin.

Golden Shiner — *Notemigonus crysoleucas*

Deep-bodied; small upturned mouth; lateral line is strongly downcurved. Olive-green back with dark stripe along midline; silver to gold along sides. Keel along belly from pelvic to anal fins. To 12 inches. Inhabits vegetated lakes, ponds, swamps and backwaters of creeks and small rivers. Range in Texas: throughout the state, due to bait-bucket releases; originally native only to eastern Texas.

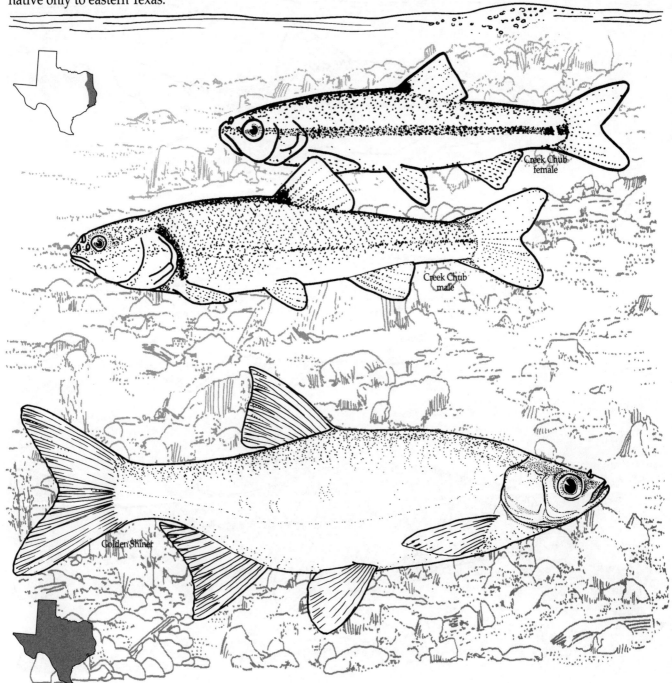

Creek Chub female

Creek Chub male

Golden Shiner

Flathead Minnow — *Pimephales promelas*

Deep, compressed body; short head, flat on top, blunt snout; short, rounded fins. Dark olive-brown above and on side; upper side has herring-bone pattern; dusky stripe along back and side; black spot at base of tail fin. Breeding male has black head, two white-gold bars along side and large breeding tubercles on snout. To 4 inches. Inhabits muddy pools of headwaters and creeks; also in ponds. Tolerant of muddy waters, heat and poor oxygen levels. Often raised in ponds for sale as bait fish. Range in Texas: statewide; extensive distribution is due to bait release.

Red Shiner — *Cyprinella lutrensis*

Deep body; rounded snout, dusty olive to blue on black-striped back; sides silvery. Breeding male has bluish body, red-orange fins (except dorsal) and orange bar behind head on sides. To 3.5 inches. Lives in silty and rocky pools and runs of creeks and small rivers. Red shiners, like all *Cyprinella* species, hide their eggs in rock crevices, and communicate with underwater sounds. Range in Texas: throughout the state.

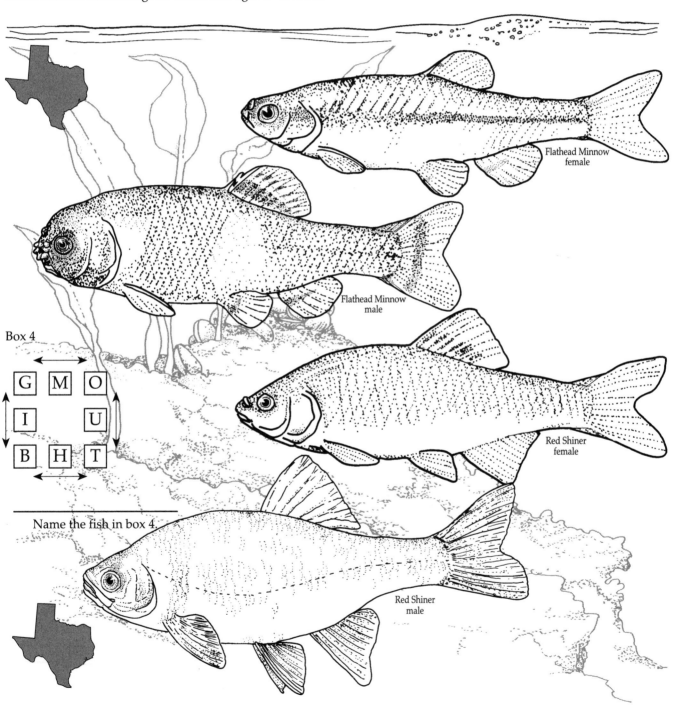

Box 4

G	M	O
I		U
B	H	T

Name the fish in box 4.

Flathead Minnow female

Flathead Minnow male

Red Shiner female

Red Shiner male

Longnose Dace — *Rhinichthys cataratae*

Long, fleshy snout extends in front of the mouth; barbel in corner of mouth. Thick caudal peduncle. Olive-brown to purple above; brown-black spots on back and side; dark stripe along side; silver to yellow below. Breeding male usually has bright red on head and fin bases. To 6.25 inches. Inhabits gravel riffles of fast creeks and small rivers; also rocky shores of lakes. Range in Texas: throughout Rio Grande drainage to Laredo.

Suckermouth Minnow — *Phenacobius mirabilis*

Long cylindrical body; Large fleshy lips on subterminal mouth. Strongly bicolored: olive-brown above, silver-white below. Thin dark stripe along side ends in intense black spot at base of tail fin. To 4.75 inches. Found in gravel riffles and runs of creeks and rivers. Range in Texas: Coastal Plains streams including Red, Sabine, Trinity and Colorado drainages.

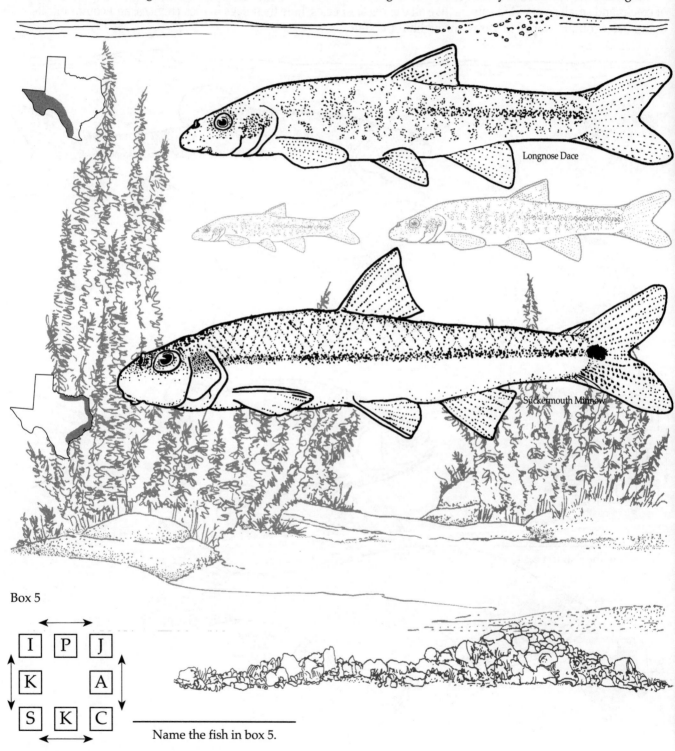

Longnose Dace

Suckermouth Minnow

Box 5

I	P	J
K		A
S	K	C

Name the fish in box 5.

50

Suckers — Family Catostomidae

Members of this family have thick lips surrounding a small mouth that usually faces downward. The jaws are toothless and all the fin rays are soft. The pelvic fins are located on the underside in the middle of the body, and the anal fin is far back. Cycloid scales cover the body and there are no scales on the head. Most suckers are bottom feeders, sucking up organic ooze, algae and small invertebrates that are then broken up by comblike pharyngeal teeth and digested in a long, coiled intestine. The majority of suckers are stream-dwelling, small to medium, streamlined forms. However, there are also large, deep-bodied suckers, such as the buffaloes and carpsuckers, that live in large rivers. The sucker family is almost entirely confined to North America with just a few Asiatic members. Of the 100 North American species, 12 are found in Texas.

Bigmouth Buffalo — *Ictiobus cyprinellus*
Deep body, with a large oval-shaped head. The terminal mouth is angled upward. Gray to olive with a coppery or greenish tint above; pale yellow to white below. Body scales are large as in carp, but buffaloes lack the barbels carp have. To 40 inches. Occurs in schools in main channels, pools and backwaters of rivers and lakes and reservoirs. Adults feed on mid-water crustaceans. Range in Texas: northeast corner of the state in the Red River below Lake Texoma and the Sulphur River.

Smallmouth Buffalo — *Ictiobus bubalus*
Deep body, with cone-shaped head. The thick-lipped mouth faces downward (unlike the terminal mouth of the bigmouth buffalo). Gray to olive above with coppery or dark blue reflections; white to yellowish below. To 13 inches. Lives in pools and main channels of rivers, lakes and reservoirs. Bottom-dweller, feeding on insect larvae and algae. Range in Texas: throughout, except the Panhandle.

Bigmouth Buffalo

Smallmouth Buffalo

Box 6

B	D	A
U		E
L	L	H

Name the fish in box 6.

River Carpsucker — *Carpioides carpis*

Deep body; small conical-shaped head with short snout. Thick-lipped, downward facing mouth. The long dorsal fin is high and pointed in front. Olive-green to bronze above; silver side; white or yellow below. To 25 inches. Inhabits pools and backwaters of rivers and reservoirs. Young fish are usually found in streams. Range in Texas: statewide.

Lake Chubsucker — *Erimyzon sucetta*

Chubby body; small nearly terminal mouth; no lateral line; high dorsal fin has rounded shape. Olive to brown above; white to yellowish below. (Young has black stripe from snout to tail fin). To 16 inches. Found over silt and debris in lakes, ponds and reservoirs. Range in Texas: eastern Texas from Red River to Brazos; also in upper Guadalupe River.

Spotted Sucker — *Minytrema melanops*

Long, streamlined body covered in parallel rows of dark spots. Small, horizontal mouth with thin lips. Dark bar on usually dished-in dorsal fin edge. Black edge on lower caudal fin. Dark green or olive-brown above; brownish side; yellowish white below. To 19.5 inches. Inhabits deep pools of streams and rivers over clay or gravel; occasionally in reservoirs. Range in Texas: primarily in eastern Texas streams and rivers from the Red to Brazos basins; an isolated population occurs in Llano River near Junction.

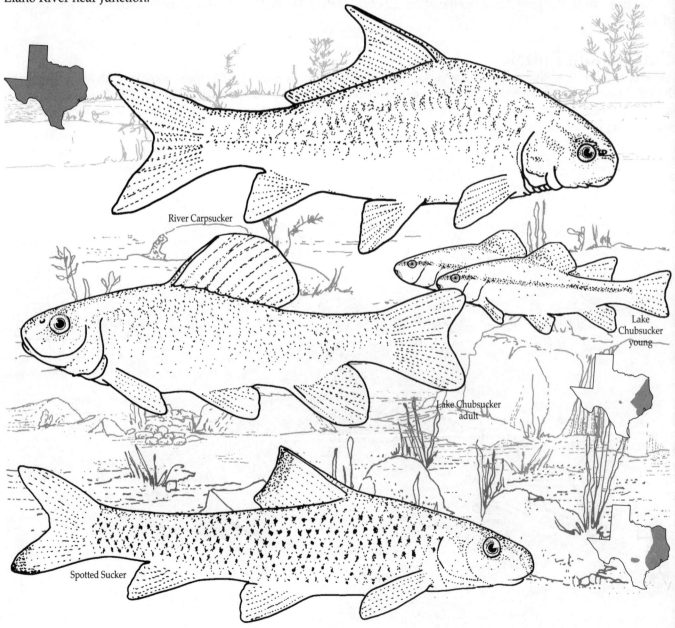

River Carpsucker

Lake Chubsucker young

Lake Chubsucker adult

Spotted Sucker

Gray Redhorse — *Moxostoma congestum*

Broad head, concave (indented) from above. Horizontal, thick-lipped mouth. Olive to yellow-gray above; light below. Yellow anal and paired fins. Breeding male is brassy gold with light orange fins. To 25.5 inches. Found in deep runs and pools of small to medium rivers; lakes. Range in Texas: streams within the Edwards Plateau including the Brazos, Colorado, Guadalupe, San Antonio, Nueces and Rio Grande drainages.

Blacktail Redhorse — *Moxostoma poecilurum*

Long, cylindrical body. Red caudal and lower fins; black stripe on lower tail fin lobe. Gold to bronze above; silver-green stripes on side; yellow to white below. To 20 inches. Found in rocky and sandy pools, runs and riffles of small to medium rivers; also in reservoirs. Range in Texas: limited to Sabine basin west through the San Jacinto drainage.

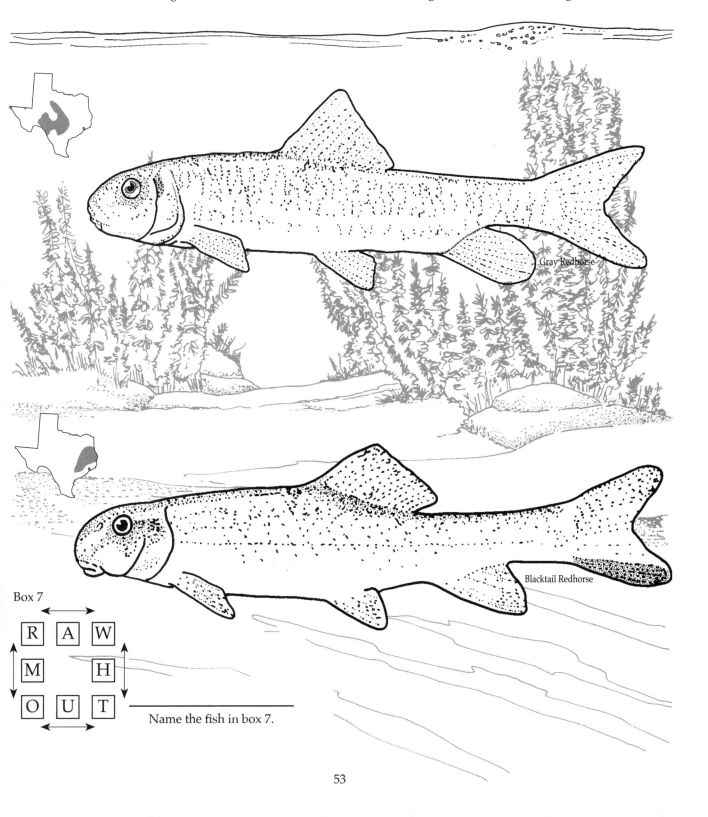

Gray Redhorse

Blacktail Redhorse

Box 7

R	A	W
M		H
O	U	T

Name the fish in box 7.

53

Bullhead Catfishes — Family Ictaluridae

Bullhead catfishes occur only in North and Central America. The United States and Canada have 40 species, of which 11 occur in Texas. (There are 30 other families of catfishes containing over 2,000 species worldwide).

Bullhead catfishes have 4 pairs of barbels around the mouth, no scales, a small adipose fin (between the dorsal and caudal fins), a wide-based anal fin and stout spines on dorsal and pectoral fins. Some, called madtoms, have poison glands surrounding the fin spines, and their "sting" can be very painful. Bullhead catfishes are mostly nocturnal, feeding near the bottom on animal and plant material.

Black Bullhead — *Ameiurus melas*
Black or dusky chin barbels. Short, rounded tail fin, only slightly notched. Dark olive brown above; light, shiny greenish side; yellow-gray to white below. To 24.5 inches. Found in pools and backwaters in creeks and rivers; also reservoirs and ponds. Both sexes excavate a nest and guard the eggs and schooling young. Range in Texas: now statewide; originally only in Trans-Pecos region.

Yellow Bullhead — *Ameiurus natalis*
White or yellow chin barbels. Rear edge of tail fin rounded or nearly straight. Large anal fin. Yellow to olive-green above; lighter on the side; bright yellow to white below. Both parents excavate nest and guard young. To 18.25 inches. Found in pools and backwaters of creeks and rivers; also in reservoirs and ponds. Range in Texas: throughout the state with the exception of the Trans-Pecos and Panhandle regions.

Black Bullhead

Yellow Bullhead

Blue Catfish — *Ictalurus furcatus*

Long, straight-edged, deeply forked tail fin with enlarged lower lobe. Long, tapered anal fin. Even slate-blue above and on upper side shading to white below. No dark spots on body except for specimens from the Rio Grande. To 65 inches. Found in deep water of large rivers; sometimes in reservoirs. Male selects nest site under logs, drift piles or empty cans. After spawning, male diligently guards eggs and developing young. Range in Texas: throughout the state except northwestern regions (including the Panhandle).

Channel Catfish — *Ictalurus punctatus*

Scattered dark spots on back and side; rounded anal fin; deeply forked tail. Upper jaw projects beyond lower jaw. Brownish to slate-blue on back and side; silver-white below. To 50 inches. Male prepares nest and guards young. Inhabits reservoirs and large streams with low or moderate current. Range in Texas: throughout the state; originally not in Upper Rio Grande and Pecos basins.

Flathead Catfish — *Pylodictis olivaris*

Slender body; wide, flat head; lower jaw projecting beyond upper jaw. White tip on upper lobe of caudal fin which is rounded or slightly notched. Yellow to brown with dark mottling above; white to yellow below. To 61 inches. Found in log-bottomed pools with slow flowing rivers; also in lakes. Male constructs nest in natural cavity and guards developing eggs. Adults feed almost exclusively on fish. Range in Texas: now statewide, but probably originally not in northern Texas.

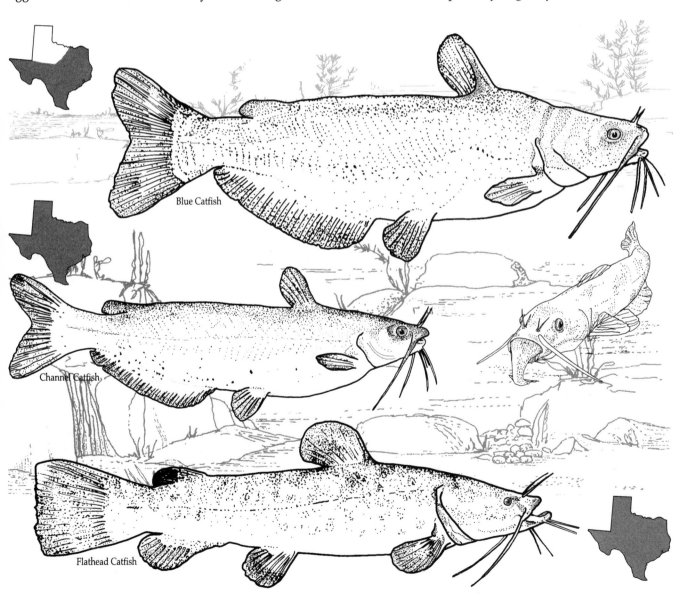

Blue Catfish

Channel Catfish

Flathead Catfish

Tadpole Madtom — *Noturus gyrinus*

Chubby body; terminal mouth with jaws of equal size. Like all madtoms, the adipose fin is long and low and joined to the tail fin. Uniform light tan body; dark gray line along the side. To 5 inches. Found in pools (usually rocky or with bottom vegetation) of lowland creeks and rivers; also in lakes. Range in Texas: throughout eastern and most of central Texas, from Red River to Nueces basin.

Widemouth Blindcat — *Satan eurystomus*

No eyes. White or pinkish overall. Broad flat head and snout. Teeth in jaws. Long adipose fin. Lateral line canals well developed. To 5.25 inches. Lives in subterranean waters at depths of 1,000 to 1,900 feet. Range in Texas: known only from five artesian wells penetrating the San Antonio Pool of the Edwards Aquifer near San Antonio. **Endangered.**

Toothless Blindcat — *Trogloglanis pattersoni*

No eyes. White or pinkish body; red mouth. No teeth in jaws. Short lower jaw curved upward into mouth. Rounded head and snout. Rear edge of adipose fin joins caudal fin. Lateral line canals on head well developed. To 4 inches. Range in Texas: known only from five artesian wells penetrating the San Antonio Pool of the Edwards Aquifer near San Antonio. **Endangered.**

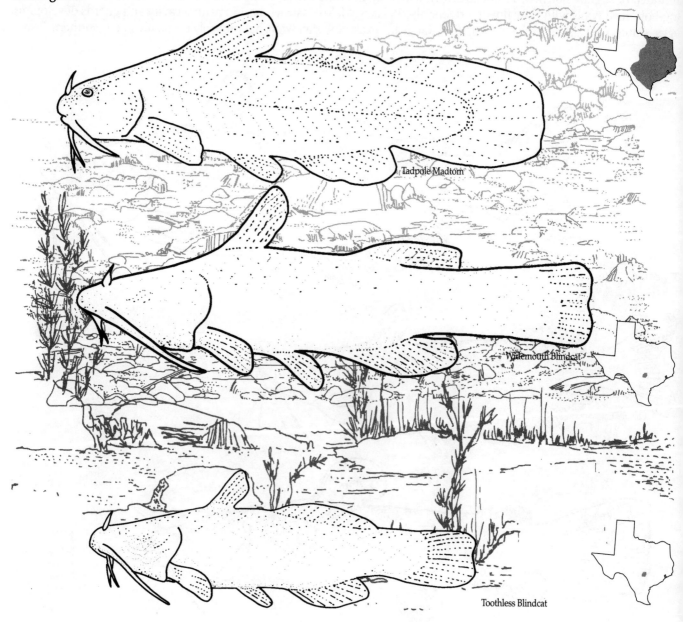

Tadpole Madtom

Widemouth Blindcat

Toothless Blindcat

56

Suckermouth Catfishes — Family Loricariidae

This group, consisting of 450 species, is native to Costa Rica, Panama and South America. Several members of this family have been imported into North America as popular aquarium fishes. At least four species have been introduced into North American waters and are reproducing. Suckermouth catfishes usually have bony plates covering the body, one pair of barbels on their warty sucking lips located on the underside and a spine in front of the adipose fin (when present). Most species are flattened below. The species introduced into Texas is commonly called "Armadillo del Rio" (or "river armadillo") and is a close relative of the popular aquarium catfish *Hypostomas plecostomas*, usually called "Plecostomas" in the trade.

Armadillo del Rio — *Hypostomas* sp.
Large bony plates above; stout spine in front of dorsal, pectoral and pelvic fins. Black or brown spots and stripes on olive-brown body and fins. To 18 inches. Found in rocky pools and runs. Range in Texas: headwaters of the San Antonio River, Bexar County and Comal Springs, Comal County.

Pirate Perch — Family Aphredoderidae

The pirate perch is the only living member of its family. It has a large mouth, ctenoid scales, a single dorsal fin with both spines and rays, and pelvic fins located far forward on the body. The anus and urogenital openings are located near the throat in the adult. It ranges widely throughout the Atlantic Slope, Gulf Coast and Mississippi Valley streams.

Pirate Perch — *Aphredoderus sayanus*

Short, deep body; large head; large mouth; lower jaw sticks out; square tail fin. Gray to black above often speckled; yellow-white below; black bar below eye; black bar on tail fin base. To 5.5 inches. Found in weedy or muddy swamps and bayous. Range in Texas: eastern Texas, from the Red River south through the lower Brazos Basin.

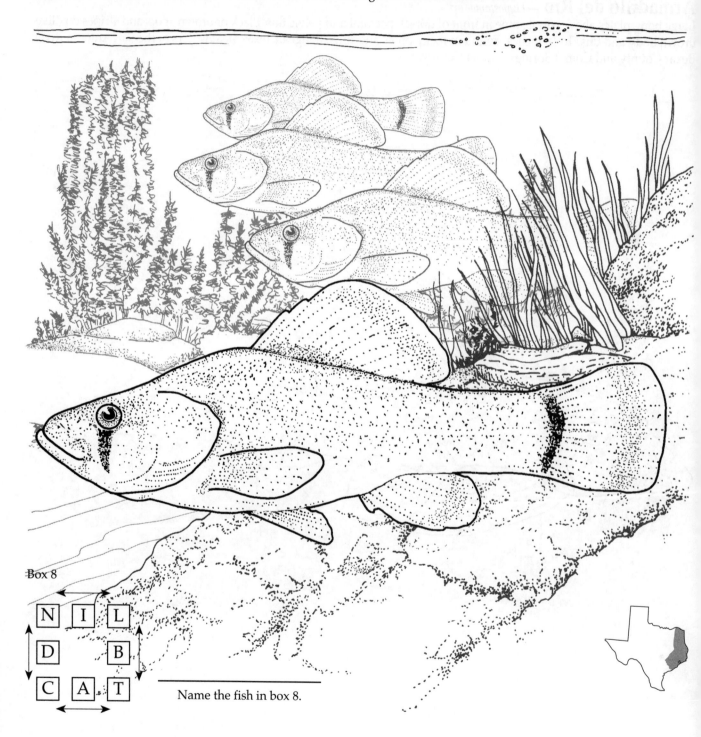

Box 8

N	I	L
D		B
C	A	T

Name the fish in box 8.

Topminnows and Killifishes — Family Fundulidae

Members of this family are small, often brightly colored fishes with a flattened head and back, upturned mouth, large head, one dorsal fin (without spines) located far back on the body, no lateral line, and pelvic fins located in the abdominal region. The family contains 40 species that live in fresh, brackish and salt water of North America and Mexico and in Bermuda and Cuba. Texas has five strictly freshwater species and seven that are mainly coastal and penetrate short distances upstream in coastal rivers. In the bait trade, killifishes are sold as chubs.

Golden Topminnow — *Fundulus chrysotus*
Golden flecks on side; from 8 to 11 green bars (often faint) on side of large male. Yellow-green above; white below. Breeding male has red or red-brown spots on rear half of body and on fins. To 3 inches. Found in swamps, sloughs and backwaters of sluggish creeks and small rivers. Range in Texas: from Sabine River south in coastal streams to the Lavaca River.

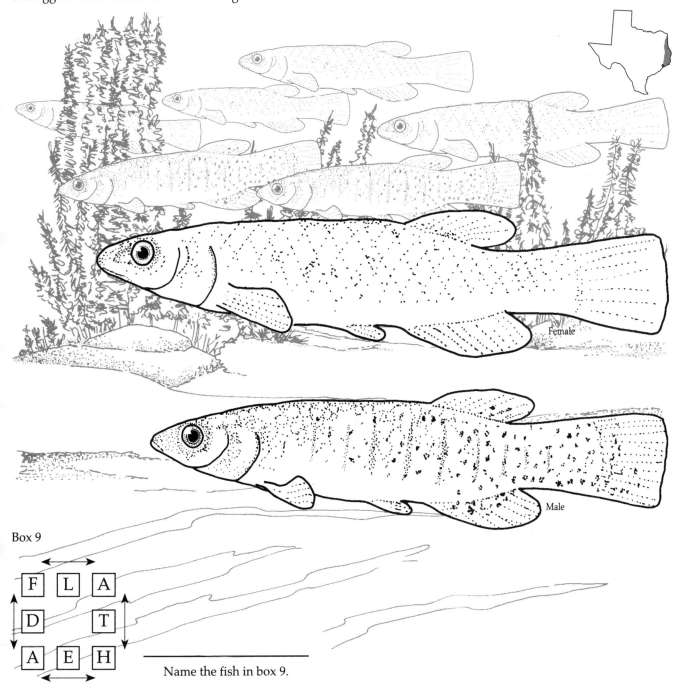

Box 9

Name the fish in box 9.

Western Starhead Topminnow — *Fundulus dispar blairae*

Large blue-black bar under eye; from seven to nine thin brownish stripes (on male) or rows of dots (on female) along side; a large iridescent gold spot on the top of head. Olive above; green, red and blue flecks on silver-yellow side; white below. Small red-brown spots on dorsal, anal and tail fin of male. To 3 inches. Found in vegetated sloughs, swamps and backwaters of streams. Range in Texas: from Red River south to Brazos River near College Station.

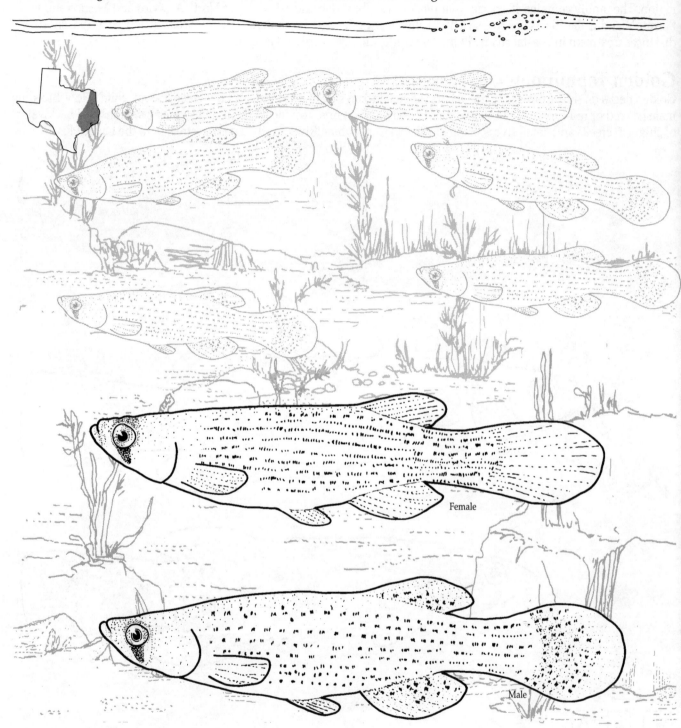

Female

Male

Blackstripe Topminnow — *Fundulus notatus*

Wide blue-black stripe along side, around snout and onto tail fin. Olive-tan above; silver-white spot on top of head; usually a few spots on upper side; light blue along upper edge of stripe; yellow, dark-spotted fins; white-yellow below. Male has cross-bars on stripe. To 3 inches. Found in quiet surface waters, near margins of creeks, small rivers and ponds. Range in Texas: eastern Texas from the Red to the San Antonio basins.

Plains Killifish — *Fundulus zebrinus*

From 12 to 26 gray-green bars on silver-white side. Breeding male has bright red fins. Tan-olive above; white to yellow below. To 4 inches. Found in shallow sandy runs, pools and backwaters of creeks and small rivers. Can survive extremely alkaline or saline streams. Buries itself in sand so that only mouth and eyes are visible. Range in Texas: occurs widely in western half of state; an introduced population occurs in the Rio Grande and its tributaries in the Big Bend region.

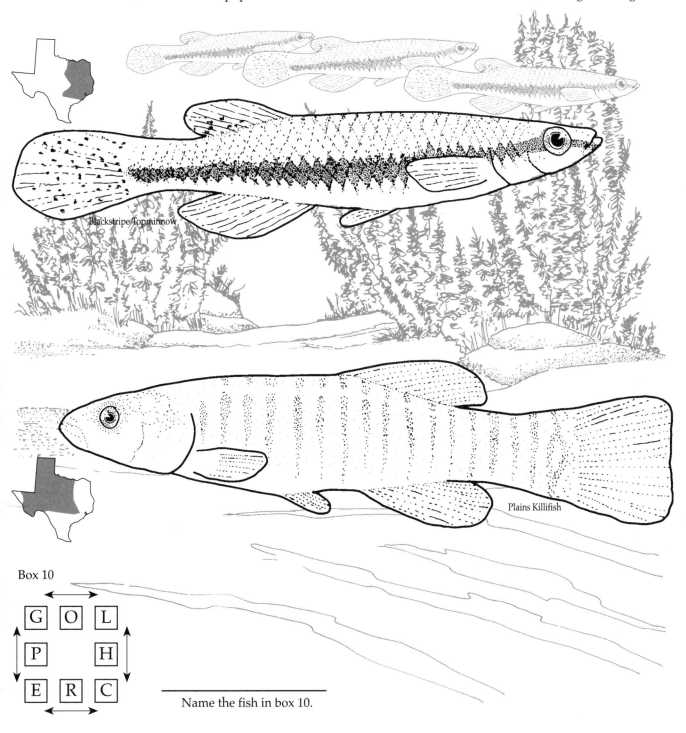

Blackstripe Topminnow

Plains Killifish

Box 10

G	O	L
P		H
E	R	C

Name the fish in box 10.

Pupfishes — Family Cyprinodontidae

The fishes in this family resemble topminnows and killifishes (family Fundulidae, see page 59) in that pupfishes are small, have upturned mouths, one dorsal fin, no lateral line, pelvic fins on the abdomen and cycloid scales. However, unlike the fundulids, pupfishes are deep bodied and most have a deep, side-to-side flattened caudal peduncle (the body region just in front of the tail fin). Pupfishes also have flattened heads on top and lightly arched backs. The family consists of about 105 species in the Americas, southeastern Eurasia and Africa. Most of North America's pupfishes live in the southwestern deserts. Texas has six species, all of which belong to the genus *Cyprinodon*. Pupfishes can survive extreme environmental conditions. They can tolerate temperatures from freezing to 113 degrees F, salinity three times that of sea water and very low oxygen concentrations.

Comanche Springs Pupfish — *Cyprinodon elegans*
A slender caudal peduncle compared to other pupfishes. Brown-black blotches form an interrupted stripe along silver side. Additional blotches on female. Gray-green above; pale yellow below. To 2.5 inches. Found in spring-fed canals and ditches, usually over mud. Range in Texas: restricted to a small series of springs, their out-flows and irrigation canals near Balmorhea, Texas, (Jeff Davis and Reeves counties); historically, the species also occurred in Comanche Springs (Pecos County) before the springs were pumped dry. **Endangered**.

Red River Pupfish — *Cyprinodon rubrofluviatilis*
Green-brown above; white below. From five to eight large triangular brown blotches along silver side; no dark blotches on lower side. Unscaled belly. Breeding male has iridescent blue nape, wide black bars on side; yellow paired fins, head and belly. To 2.25 inches. Found in shallow, shady pools and runs of headwaters, creeks and small rivers. Often in very shallow and hot water. Range in Texas: occurs naturally in upper Red and Brazos river basins; also introduced in the Canadian and Colorado basins.

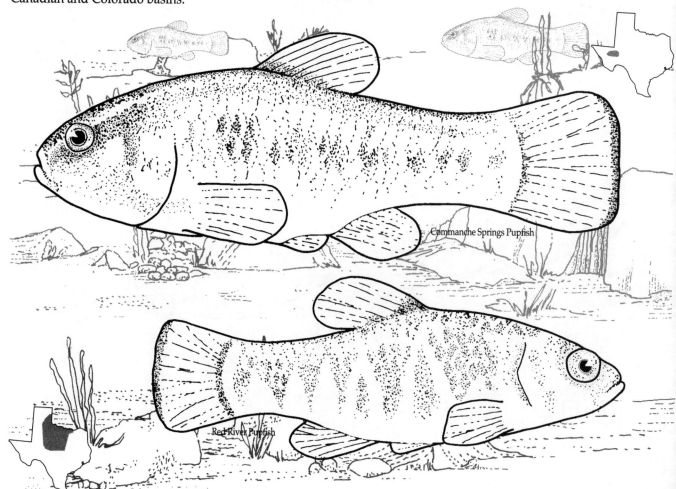

Commanche Springs Pupfish

Red River Pupfish

Sheepshead Minnow — *Cyprinodon variegatus*

Very deep-bodied, from five to eight triangular shaped dark gray bars wide on top along silvery olive side. Green to blue gray above; dark brown blotches on the rear half of upper side; white below. Breeding male is blue above and has wide dark gray bars along side; salmon cheek and belly; orangey fins. As in all pupfish breeding males, black edge on tail fin. To 3 inches. Found in salt, brackish and fresh water; usually near vegetation. Commonly sold for bait. Range in Texas: originally only Gulf Coast waters and lower reaches of coastal streams. (However, bait-bucket releases have introduced this fish into the Trans-Pecos region and San Antonio basin. Interbreeding of introduced sheepshead minnows with Trans-Pecos pupfishes has led to near extermination of several species).

Livebearers — Family Poecilidae

Male fishes of this New World family have the front rays of their anal fin elongated and modified into an organ (called gonopodium) used to accomplish internal fertilization. Females (with one exception) give birth to live young. Except for these two characteristics, live bearers resemble killifishes (see page 59) in that they have a flattened head, a strongly upturned mouth, no lateral line, one dorsal fin and pelvic fins located on the abdomen. Some populations of live bearers consist only of females (for example, the Amazon molly, see below). There are 150 species of livebearers, most of which live in the tropics. Texas has 13 species.

Amazon Molly — *Poecilia formosa*
Small head; deep compressed body; very deep caudal peduncle. Olive above; white to yellow below; sometimes has rows of dusky black spots on side. To 3.75 inches. Found in backwaters and quiet pools of streams, sloughs, and ditches in fresh and brackish water. This is an all-female species. Range in Texas: native to lower Rio Grande; introduced in the lower Nueces, San Antonio and San Marcos rivers.

Sailfin Molly — *Poecilia latipinna*
Small head; deep body; deep caudal peduncle. Five rows of dark brown spots and yellow flecks on olive side. Olive above; yellowish below; brown spots on dorsal and caudal fins. Large male has huge sail-like dorsal fin with orange edge and rows of dark spots; iridescent blue back; orange on lower head and breast. To 6 inches. Found in ponds, lakes and quiet backwaters and pools of streams and in fresh and brackish water. Range in Texas: coastal waters and lower Rio Grande, introduced in spring-fed Central Texas headwaters.

Amazon Molly

Sailfin Molly male

Sailfin Molly female

Western Mosquitofish — *Gambusia affinis*

Large dusky to black "teardrop" (a vertical line below eye). One to three rows of black spots on dorsal and tail fins. Light olive-gray to yellow-brown above; dark stripe along back to dorsal fin; shimmering yellow and bluish on silver-gray side. Black spot near anus on pregnant female. To 2.5 inches. Found in standing and slow-moving water in vegetated ponds, lakes and backwaters. Often in brackish waters. Range in Texas: throughout state. (Has been widely introduced throughout the world for mosquito control.)

Big Bend Gambusia — *Gambusia gaigei*

Prominent black spots and crescents on upper side; dark stripe along side. Dusky "teardrop". Golden olive above; dark stripe along back to dorsal fin. Dark anal spot on female. Large male has orange snout; red-orange on dorsal and tail fins. To 2.25 inches. Lives in vegetated, spring-fed sloughs and ponds. Range in Texas: formerly two natural springs in Brewster County. Now restricted to an artificial spring-fed pond in Big Bend National Park. **Endangered**.

Largespring Gambusia — *Gambusia geiseri*

Distinct row of black spots on middle of dorsal and caudal fins (sometimes with additional faint rows). Scattered black spots on side. Olive above; dark stripe along back to dorsal fin; shimmering blue and yellow on silvery side. No tear drop; no anal spot. To 1.75 inches. Found in large springs. Range in Texas: originally restricted to the headwaters of the San Marcos and Comal rivers in Central Texas. Now introduced into the headwaters of the Concho River (Tom Green County), San Solomon Springs (Reeves County), Leon Creek (Pecos County) and Independence Creek (Terrell County).

Western Mosquitofish

Big Bend Gambusia

Largespring Gambusia

Silversides — Family Atherinidae

Members of this worldwide family are small fishes living originally around the shore areas of tropical, subtropical and, to some extent, temperate areas. They are silvery, translucent and strongly flattened from side-to-side. Silversides have scales on the head, large eyes, an upturned terminal mouth, a long snout, no lateral line, a sickle-shaped anal fin and pelvic fins situated on the abdomen. They can be readily distinguished from the minnow group by their having two widely separated dorsal fins, the front one being small and with spines.

Silversides usually occur in large schools near the surface. They often leave the water and glide through the air for short distances when spawning or disturbed. Of the 160 species in this family, only three occur in the fresh waters of North America. Two of these are found in Texas.

Brook Silverside — *Labidesthes sicculus*
Long beak-like snout. Two widely separated dorsal fins, the first small and with spines. Pale green above; scales faintly outlined; bright silver stripe along side. Breeding male has red snout, bright yellow-green body. To 5 inches. Occurs near surface of lakes, ponds and quiet pools of creeks and rivers. Range in Texas: restricted to Sabine and portions of Red River of eastern Texas.

Inland Silverside — *Menidia beryllina*
Snout more rounded and shorter than brook silverside (see above). Two widely separated dorsal fins, the first small and with spines. Pale yellow-green above; scales faintly outlined; bright silver stripe along side. To 6 inches. Found at surface of clear, quiet waters over sand and gravel. Range in Texas: originally in coastal waters and upstream in coastal river systems along Gulf including Rio Grande as far as the Pecos River drainage; widely introduced in Texas reservoirs as forage for sport fishes.

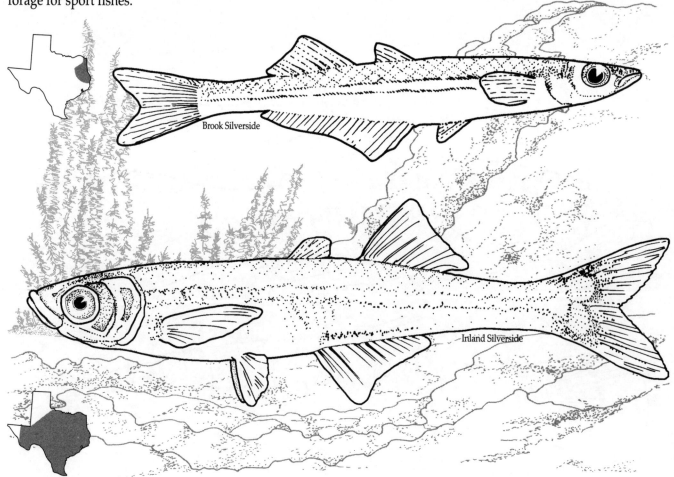

Brook Silverside

Inland Silverside

Temperate Basses — Family Moronidae

Family members are moderate-to-large, side-to-side flattened, deep-bodied fishes. They have two dorsal fins, the first with spines (usually nine) and the second with one spine up front and about 12 rays behind it. The anal fin also has spines in front. One or two sharp points stick out from the back edge of the gill cover. Temperate basses are very popular sport fishes and various species occur in North America, Europe and northern Africa. Of the four North American species, three are found in Texas.

White Bass — *Morone chrysops*

Four to seven gray-brown stripes on silver-white side. Dorsal fins separated. Body deepest between dorsal fins. Blue-gray above; white below. Two sharp points on gill cover. Teeth in single patch on back of tongue. To 17.5 inches. Found in lakes and ponds, and pools of rivers. Adults usually found in schools. Spawning occurs on surface or in mid water. Fertilized eggs sink to the bottom. Gizzard and threadfin shad are preferred food items, along with crustaceans and insects. Range in Texas: originally in drainages from the Red River to the Rio Grande; now widely introduced into reservoirs.

White Bass

67

Yellow Bass — *Morone mississippiensis*

Five to seven black stripes on silver-yellow side, with the lowermost stripe broken and offset. Dorsal fins united at base. Olive-gray above; yellow-white below. No teeth on tongue. Back of gill cover has a single point. To 18 inches. Found in pools and backwaters of rivers; also lakes. Range in Texas: eastern Texas from the Red River southward to San Jacinto drainage.

Striped Bass — *Morone saxatilis*

Shape is more elongated than in other temperate basses. Six to nine dark-gray stripes on silver-white side. Dorsal fins separate. Dark olive to deep gray above, silvery side has brassy flecks. (Young lack stripes, have dusky bar instead). Teeth in two parallel patches on the back of the tongue. Two points on back edge of gill cover. To 79 inches. Marine, but ascends large rivers far upstream to spawn. Range in Texas: not native, but widely stocked in many reservoirs, especially Lake Texoma, where self-sustaining, successfully reproducing populations exist.

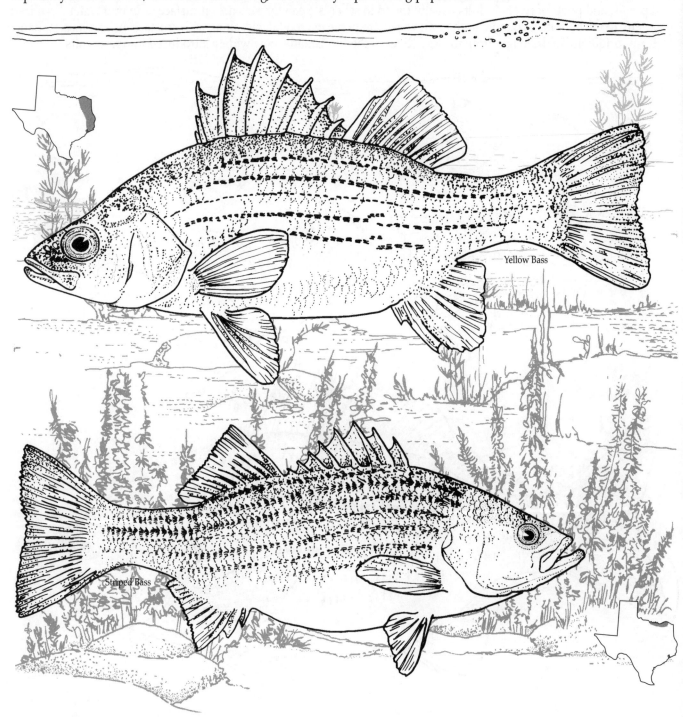

Yellow Bass

Striped Bass

68

Bony Fishes — Class Osteichthyes

Sunfishes and Basses — Family Centrarchidae

The 30 species of this family are native only to North American fresh waters. Because of the great sport fishing popularity of species such as crappies and basses, they have been introduced into parts of North America where they did not occur originally, and also into Europe and Africa. Sunfishes and basses are deep-bodied, side-to-side flattened fishes with two broadly joined dorsal fins; the lower front one with spines, and the higher second fin with rays. The pelvic fins are far forward (on the thorax). Unlike the temperate basses, there is no point on the back of the gill cover. Males of this family all construct circular pit nests of gravel and guard eggs and young. Texas has 18 species.

Flier — *Centrarchus macropterus*
Large black "teardrop" (a vertical line below eye). Interrupted rows of black spots along side. Deep, compressed body; small mouth. Dusky gray back; silver side with many green and bronze flecks. (Young have four dark bars on side). To 7.5 inches. Found in swamps, vegetated lakes, sloughs and backwaters of creeks and small rivers. Range in Texas: lowland streams in eastern Texas including the Sabine, Neches and San Jacinto drainages.

Banded Pygmy Sunfish — *Elassoma zonatum*
One to two large black spots on upper side. Seven to 12 dark green to blue-black bars on side. No scales on top of head. No lateral line. (This characteristic has caused some biologists to place this and similar species in a separate family, the pygmy sunfishes.) Breeding male is black with green-gold flecks and alternating gold and black bars on side. To 1.75 inches. Lives in swamps, sloughs and small, sluggish streams. Range in Texas: eastern Texas from Red River southward to the Brazos River basin.

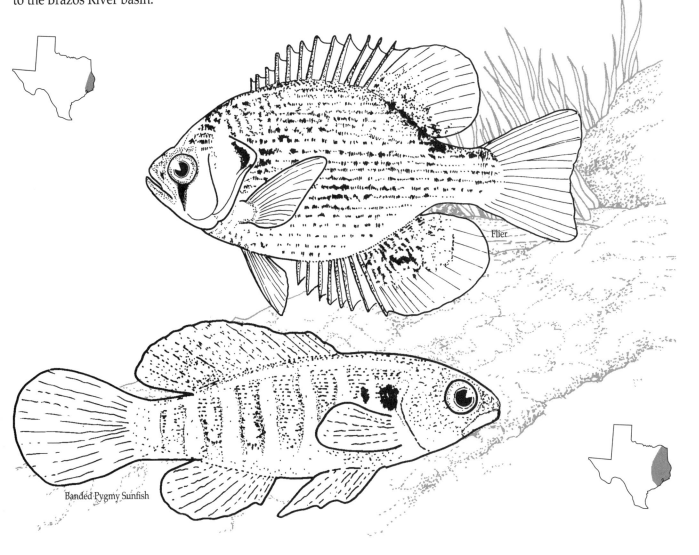

Flier

Banded Pygmy Sunfish

Green Sunfish — *Lepomis cyanellus*

Large mouth with upper jaw extending beyond eye pupil. Adult has large black spot at rear of second dorsal and anal fin bases. Fairly slender, thick body. Blue-green back and side, often with yellow metallic green flecks; sometimes dusky bars on side. "Ear flap" at rear of gill cover is black and edged in yellowish white. To 12 inches. Inhabits quiet pools and backwaters of sluggish streams, lakes and ponds near vegetation. Able to tolerate a wide range of environmental conditions. Range in Texas: throughout the state.

Warmouth — *Lepomis gulosus*

Fairly slender thick body. Large mouth. Dark red brown lines (absent in young) radiate from back of red eye. Patch of teeth on tongue (detect by feeling with finger). Olive-brown above; dark brown mottling on back and upper side; red spot (in adult) behind yellow edge of short "ear flap"; cream to yellow below. Breeding male has bright red-orange spot on base of second dorsal fin. To 12 inches. Found in vegetated lakes, ponds, swamps and quiet stream waters. Range in Texas: statewide except plains streams in Texas Panhandle; most abundant in east.

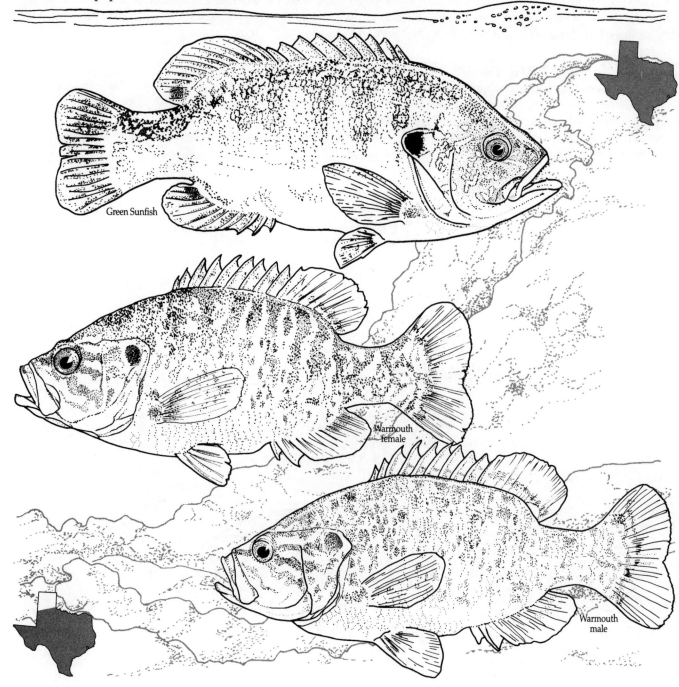

Green Sunfish

Warmouth female

Warmouth male

70

Bluegill — *Lepomis macrochirus*
Relatively small mouth; deep extremely compressed body. Large black spot at rear of second dorsal fin. Dark bars (absent in turbid water) along upper side. Long pointed pectoral fin. "Ear flap" is solid black. Olive back and side with yellow and green flecks; adult with overall blue sheen; white to yellow below. Breeding male has blue head; bright red-orange breast and belly. To 16.25 inches. Inhabits vegetated lakes, ponds, swamps and pools of creeks and rivers. Range in Texas: statewide.

Longear Sunfish — *Lepomis megalotis*
Especially long black "ear flap" trimmed in white in adult. Wavy blue lines on cheek region. Adult is dark red above; orange below, marbled and speckled with blue. To 9.5 inches. Found in rocky or sandy pools of headwaters, creeks and small rivers. Range in Texas: throughout, except for headwaters of Brazos and Canadian rivers.

Redear Sunfish — *Lepomis microlophus*
Red or orange edge on black "ear flap". Long pointed pectoral fin. Pointed snout with relatively small mouth. Dark olive green above; yellowish green side; orange-white below. To 10 inches. Inhabits vegetated ponds, swamps, lakes and pools of small rivers. Range in Texas: native to eastern two-thirds; now introduced throughout state.

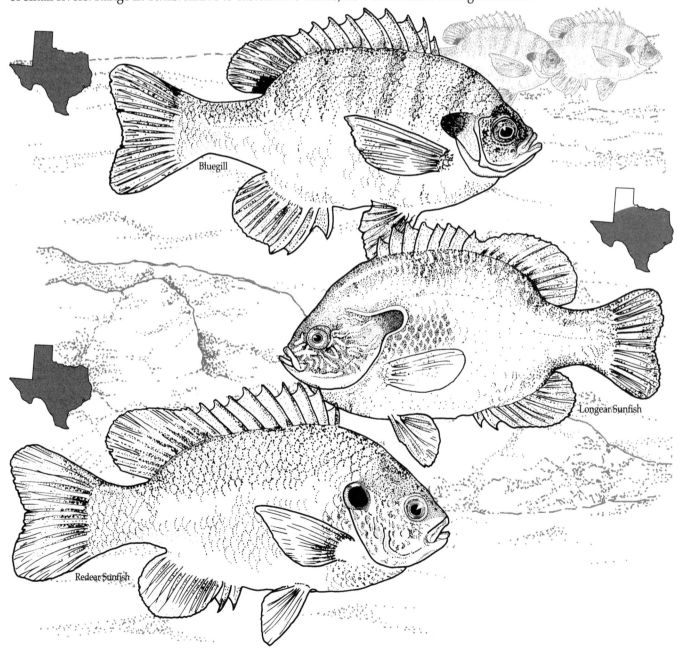

Bluegill

Longear Sunfish

Redear Sunfish

Largemouth Bass — *Micropterus salmoides*

Dorsal fin almost divided into separate spiny and soft-rayed portions. Very large mouth; upper jaw extending well past eye. Silver to brassy green above; dark olive mottling; broad black stripe (often broken up into blotches) along side as far as the eye; white below. To 25 inches. Found in clear, vegetated lakes, swamps and backwaters of creeks and rivers. Common in reservoirs. Range in Texas: throughout state; except Panhandle; stocked widely in reservoirs.

Smallmouth Bass — *Micropterus dolomieu*

Dark brown, bronze specks often joined into about 12 bars on yellow-green side. Olive above; dark mottling on back and side; red eye. Yellow-white below. Large mouth, but unlike the largemouth bass, upper jaw extends only as far as eye. To 16 inches. Found in large and deep clear-water lakes and cool gravel-bottomed streams. Range in Texas: not native; now stocked in many areas, especially streams of the Edwards Plateau.

Spotted Bass — *Micropterus punctulatus*

Rows of small black spots on lower side; black stripe (or series of partly joined blotches) along side. Gold-green above; dark olive mottling; yellow-white below. Large mouth; upper jaw extends under rear half of eye. To 15 inches. Found in clear, gravelly flowing pools and runs of creeks and small rivers; also in reservoirs. Range in Texas: portions of eastern Texas from Guadalupe basin to Red River, but not including the Edwards Plateau.

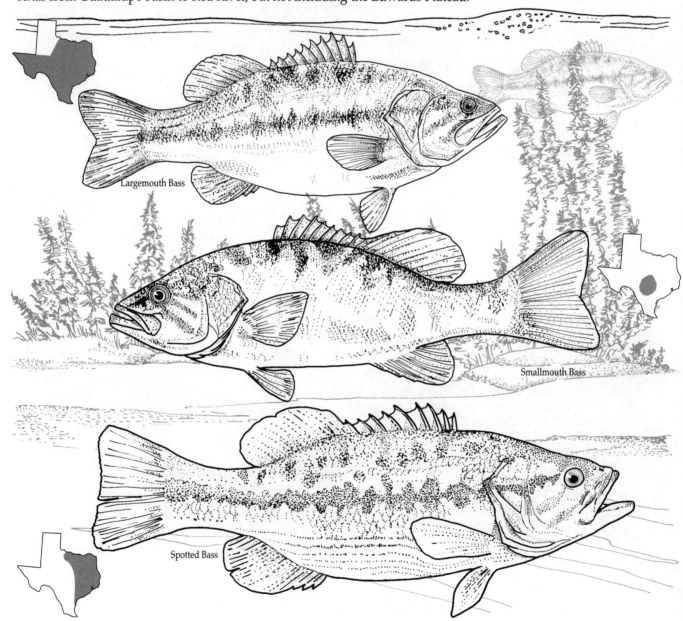

Largemouth Bass

Smallmouth Bass

Spotted Bass

Guadalupe Bass — *Micropterus treculi*

Similar to spotted bass, but instead of conjoined side blotches these blotches form about 12 bars that extend lower than any markings in smallmouth or spotted bass. Greenish above; yellow-white below. To 15 inches. Found in gravel riffles, runs and flowing pools of creeks and small rivers. Range in Texas: native to streams of northern and eastern Edwards Plateau of the Brazos, Colorado, Guadalupe and San Antonio basins; also in lower Colorado River and introduced in Nueces River. State Fish of Texas.

White Crappie — *Pomoxis annularis*

Arched portion of body in front of dorsal fin is relatively long, with a sharp dip over eye. Large mouth; upper jaw extends under eye. Deep, extremely compressed body. Gray-green above; silver side with six to nine dusky, chain like bars on side; white below. To 14 inches. Found in sand and mud-bottomed turbid pools and backwaters of creeks and rivers; also lakes. Range in Texas: native to eastern two-thirds of state; introduced statewide except for upper portions of Rio Grande and Pecos drainages.

Black Crappie — *Pomoxis nigromaculatus*

Body shape similar to White Crappie (see above), but somewhat deeper body. Gray-green above, silver side with irregular black lines and blotches; no bars. Like the white crappie, breeding male develops dark coloration in the throat region. To 12 inches. Found usually in clear acidic waters among vegetation in lakes, ponds, sloughs and in backwaters of streams. Range in Texas: native to central and eastern portions of the state, except for Edwards Plateau; now widely introduced throughout.

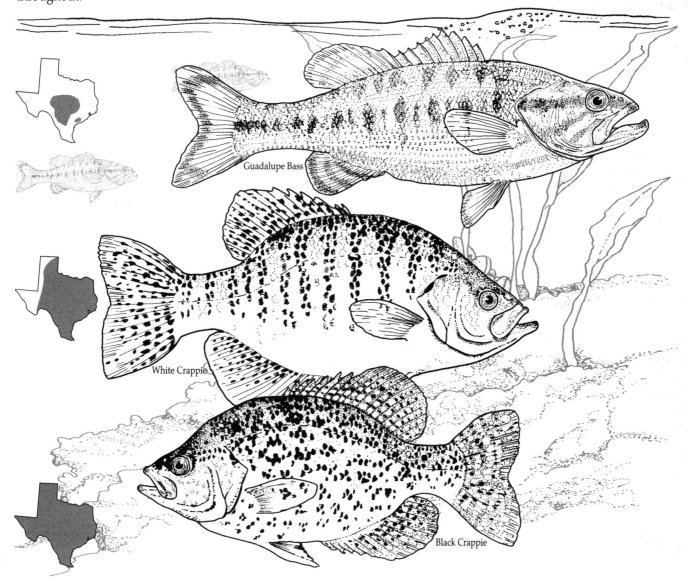

Guadalupe Bass

White Crappie

Black Crappie

Perches: Darters, Walleye and Sauger — Family Percidae

With about 150 species, this is the second most diverse family (after the cyprinids or minnows) of North American freshwater fishes. Most percids are darters. Darters are small (usually under 4 inches) and often colorful, especially the breeding males. Most have lost their air-bladders and spend their time darting about the bottom of streams and lakes, eating small crustaceans and insects. Family characteristics include: two dorsal fins, separate or slightly joined, the first with spines, the second with rays; pelvic fins located far forward on the thorax, and ctenoid scales. Other than darters, the family includes the North American walleye, sauger and yellow perch, and 14 European perches. Texas has 21 native species, all of them darters.

Walleye — *Stizostedion vitreum*
Long slender body. Very large mouth extending beyond middle of filmed-over, silvery eye. Large black spot on rear of first dorsal fin. Yellow-olive to brown above; brassy yellow side; five to 12 indistinct saddles extend faintly onto side; white below. White tip on lower lobe of forked tail fin. Numerous sharp teeth in the jaws and on the roof of the mouth. Eggs are scattered at random and fertilized. There is no nest building or parental care. To 36 inches. Found in clear water in lakes; also pools and backwaters of rivers. Range in Texas: not native; stocked in numerous reservoirs as a popular sport fish; breeds in northern Texas lakes, such as Lake Meredith.

Sauger — *Stizostedion canadense*
Similar to the walleye (see above) but has many half-moon markings on first dorsal fin and no black spot. There are fewer saddles than on walleye and no white tip on lower tail fin. To 30 inches. Found in sandy and muddy pools and backwaters of rivers; also lakes and reservoirs. Range in Texas: not native; introduced to a few reservoirs in northern Texas.

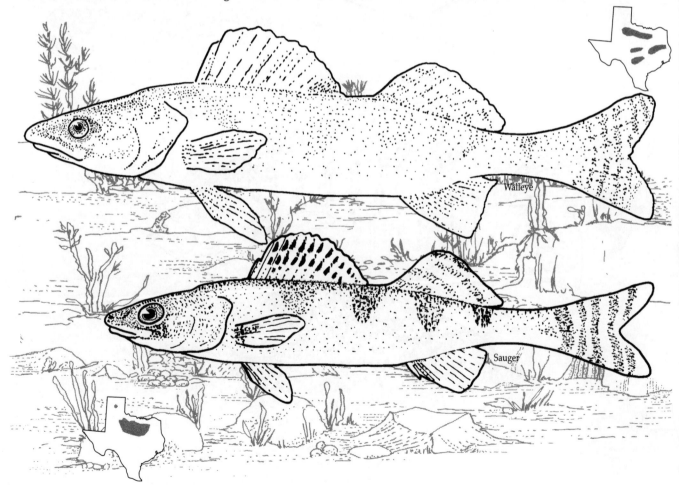

The two species below belong to the *Percina* genus which is considered primitive. These darters retain a small air-bladder and spend more time off the bottom than other darters. Also, they have a complete lateral line and scutes (heavy scales) on the breast in both sexes and along the midline of the belly of the male (see drawing below).

Bigscale Logperch — *Percina macrolepida*
Light colored with small head. 15 to 20 long, dark bars along side extend over back joining those of the other side. Olive to yellow above; white below. Scales on top of head. Dusky spot under eye. To 4.5 inches. Inhabits gravel and sand runs and pools of small to medium rivers; also reservoirs. Range in Texas: from Red and Sabine basins in eastern Texas south and west to the Devils River (Rio Grande drainage).

Dusky Darter — *Percina sciera*
Olive to dusky black above; eight to nine brown saddles on back; wavy dark lines on upper side; row of oval black blotches along side. To 5 inches. Found in gravel runs and riffles of creeks and small rivers. Range in Texas: from Guadalupe River system north and east to Red and Sabine rivers.

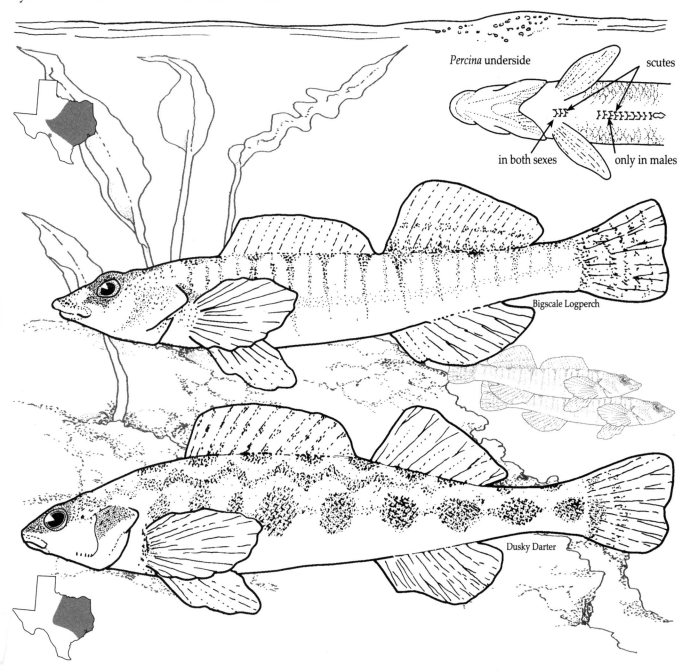

Percina underside

scutes

in both sexes

only in males

Bigscale Logperch

Dusky Darter

The following darter species belong to the *Etheostoma*, the largest genus of North American fishes. Some of these are spectacularly colorful. Species of *Etheostoma* do not have the underside scutes common to members of the genus *Percina* (see above).

Scaly Sand Darter — *Etheostoma vivax*
Vertical dark green blotches along side. Both dorsal fins have dusky edge and middle band. Dark green blotches along back. To 2.25 inches. Inhabits sandy runs of creeks and small rivers. Range in Texas: eastern Texas from San Jacinto to Sabine rivers.

Mud Darter — *Etheostoma asprigene*
Dark bars on side, blue between dull orange in male, duller in female. Fully scaled cheek. First dorsal fin has middle red band, blue edge and base, large black blotch at rear. Olive-brown above, six to 10 dark saddles, white-orange below. Large dusky "teardrop". Middle red band on second dorsal in male. To 2.75 inches. Inhabits sluggish riffles over rocks or debris in river; lowland lakes. Range in Texas: eastern Texas from the Red River south to Neches basin.

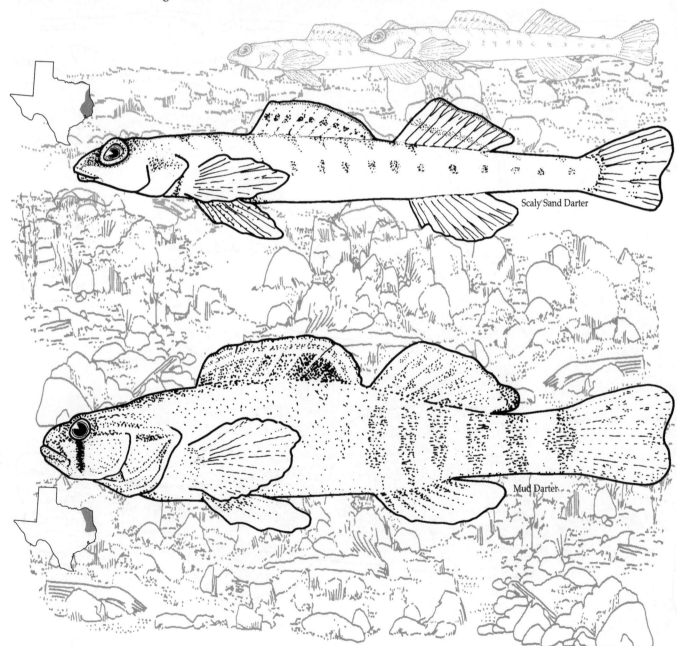

Scaly Sand Darter

Mud Darter

Slough Darter — *Etheostoma gracile*

Yellow above; green saddle and wavy lines on back; bright green bars on side of male; green squares or mottling on female; yellow to white below. Middle red band on first dorsal fin. Thin "teardrop". To 2.25 inches. Found in slow flowing or standing water over mud. Range in Texas: Gulf Coast Plain from Red River to Rio Grande.

Rio Grande Darter — *Etheostoma grahami*

Relatively deep bodied. Many small red (on male) or black (on female) spots on side. Red first dorsal fin. Olive above, eight to 10 dark saddles, dusky blotches along side; white-yellow below. Faint "teardrop". To 2.25 inches. Inhabits gravel riffles of creeks and small rivers. Range in Texas: mainstream and spring-fed tributaries of the Rio Grande and lower Pecos River downstream to Devils River and Dolan, San Felipe and Sycamore creeks. **Threatened**.

Slough Darter

Rio Grande Darter

Greenthroat Darter — *Etheostoma lepidum*

Red-orange specks or spots between long green bars on side of male; yellow between short brown-black bars on female. Olive above; dark saddles; white to orange below. Three black spots on base of tail fin. Thin black "teardrop". To 2.5 inches. Inhabits spring-fed streams and vegetated riffles of headwaters, creeks and small rivers. Range in Texas: Edwards Plateau streams, especially headwaters from the Colorado River southward to Nueces River basin.

Orangethroat Darter — *Etheostoma spectabile*

Dark bars on side. (Bars are blue between orange on male; brown between yellow-white on female). First dorsal fin is orange with blue border. Dusky "teardrop". Olive to brown with dark saddles above orange to white below. Larger male has blue anal and pelvic fins. To 2.75 inches. Lives in shallow gravel riffles and rocky pools of headwaters, creeks and small rivers. Range in Texas: primarily on Edwards Plateau from San Antonio River north and east to Red River; does not occur on the Coastal Plain.

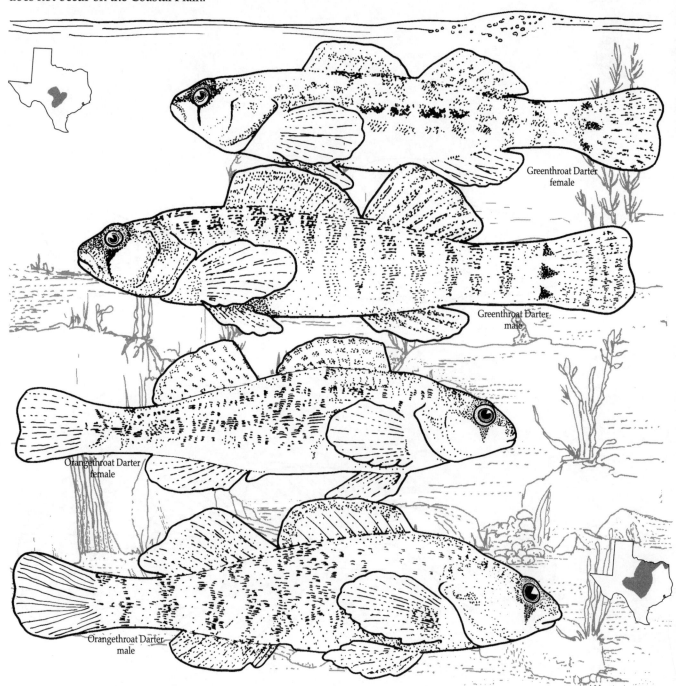

Greenthroat Darter
female

Greenthroat Darter
male

Orangethroat Darter
female

Orangethroat Darter
male

78

Drums or Croakers — Family Sciaenidae

Texas waters include the only freshwater member of this large, essentially marine family of about 210 species. Most drums are found on continental shelves of tropic and temperate regions. Drums, also called croakers, are so called because they can make sounds using their air-bladder as a resonating chamber. Family characteristics include: two joined dorsal fins, the first one short and with spines, and the second longer and with rays; a lateral line that goes to the end of the tail fin; pelvic fins placed far forward on the thorax, and ctenoid scales.

Freshwater Drum — *Aplodinotus grunniens*
Deep body, strongly arched toward the front. Silver above and on side. Rounded tail fin comes to a point in the middle. Outer pelvic fin has a long filament. To 35 inches. Found on bottom of medium to large rivers and lakes. This species is the only North American freshwater fish that produces eggs and embryos that float at the water's surface. Range in Texas: most of the state, with the exception of the Panhandle and most of the Trans Pecos regions.

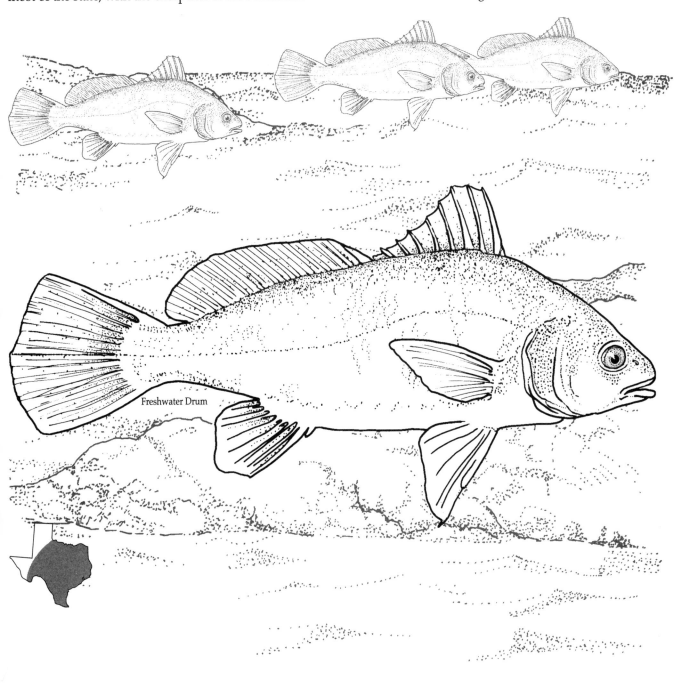

Freshwater Drum

Cichlids — Family Cichlidae

Members of this family are best known from the pet trade where they are sold as popular aquarium fishes. In the New World, cichlids are native to South America, the West Indies and Central America, with one species extending north into Texas. Cichlids also occur in Africa, Madagascar, the Middle East and India. Most cichlids are freshwater; a few live in brackish water. The family includes about 680 species, with Texas having one native species and three introduced species from Africa. Cichlids are characterized by having only one nostril on each side (most fishes have two). They also have a lateral line broken into two portions, with the front part higher than the rear part.

Rio Grande Cichlid — *Cichlasoma cyanoguttatum*
Deep bodied, with single dorsal fin, spines in front and rays towards the rear. Four to six dark elongated blotches along rear half of side. Many white and blue spots or wavy lines along side. (When breeding, body becomes white in front and black towards rear.) Black blotch on caudal fin base. To 12 inches. Found in pools and runs of warm vegetated rivers. Range in Texas: originally native only to the lower Rio Grande drainage; now introduced on Edwards Plateau.

Mozambique Tilapia — *Tilapia mossambicus*
Pointed head rising sharply over eye. Large downward slanting mouth reaches under eye. Gray to olive above; three to four black spots on yellowish gray-green side; yellow below. Large breeding male has bluish black body, white underside of head, and red pectoral fin. To 15.25 inches. Found in warm weedy pools of sluggish streams, canals, ponds; also in reservoirs. Range in Texas: introduced from southeast Africa; established in San Marcos, Guadalupe and San Antonio rivers along Balcones Fault zone; also in reservoirs.

Rio Grande Cichlid

Mozambique Tilapia

Fish Seek and Find

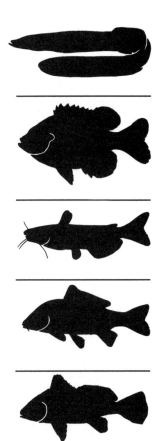

W	E	H	K	C	C	R	E	T	R	A	D	L	G	G	E	H	B
H	K	D	A	L	E	R	E	K	C	I	P	A	A	N	E	S	L
I	I	R	B	H	B	H	R	A	E	D	E	R	M	I	L	I	A
T	P	U	U	L	S	T	R	I	P	E	R	G	B	L	U	F	C
E	F	M	F	I	U	D	A	Y	N	A	A	E	U	N	B	E	K
B	O	W	F	I	N	E	E	G	D	S	I	M	S	S	B	L	B
A	L	N	A	N	F	L	G	I	O	M	N	O	I	S	L	D	A
S	U	A	L	B	N	C	L	I	I	S	B	U	A	A	A	D	S
S	P	O	O	I	O	H	E	R	L	I	O	T	P	B	C	A	S
T	O	O	R	T	C	K	I	R	K	L	W	H	R	E	K	P	H
C	I	B	T	I	B	R	O	C	K	V	T	B	I	P	C	K	E
A	A	L	C	T	J	A	M	A	L	E	R	A	E	U	R	C	E
J	O	T	A	G	E	E	C	G	I	R	O	S	Y	L	A	A	P
R	D	O	F	P	Z	D	M	O	M	S	U	S	E	A	P	J	S
D	A	C	E	I	I	T	B	I	L	I	T	A	L	D	P	P	H
R	E	N	I	H	S	A	O	S	I	D	R	H	L	A	I	I	E
M	O	P	E	R	C	H	O	H	A	E	A	T	A	U	E	K	A
F	L	A	T	H	E	A	D	M	I	N	N	O	W	G	I	S	D

Find the words in the puzzle list. They can be forward or backward or diagonal.

BLACK BASS
BLACK CRAPPIE
BLUEGILL
BOWFIN
BUFFALO
CARP
CATFISH
CICHLID
DACE
DARTER
DRUM
EEL
FLATHEAD MINNOW
GAMBUSIA
GAR
GUADALUPE BASS

PADDLEFISH
PERCH
PICKEREL
PIKE
RAINBOW TROUT
REDEAR
SHEEPSHEAD
SHINER
SILVERSIDE
SKIPJACK
SUNFISH
TILAPIA
WHITE BASS
WALLEYE

Make Sunfish (Bream) Chowder

Here is a recipe for dealing with the many small sunfish (bream) you sometimes catch with hook and worm from the end of a pier.

Instead of trying to clean and fry these small fish — which is a real chore — the best way to enjoy them is to make a hearty soup called a bream chowder.

Start by skinning each side of the fish from the gills to the tail. Next, fillet out the two slivers of meat that lie above and below the midline, from gills to tail, on each side.

Accumulate these pieces of fish (by storing them with a little water in a bag in the freezer) until you have enough to make a pot of bream chowder.

The ingredients you'll need are listed below:

Dr. Field's Bream Chowder

1/4 pound margarine or butter
2 cups chopped onion
4 tablespoons flour
2 cups water
3 cups diced raw potatoes
1 cup chopped celery
1 cup chopped raw carrots
1-pound can creamed corn
4 cups milk
1 quart, more or less, bream fillets cut to less than bite size, or as desired
1 to 2 ounces oil, margarine or butter for cooking the fish
2 teaspoons salt
2 teaspoons parsley flakes
1/2 teaspoon basil leaves
1/4 to 1/2 teaspoon garlic powder
1 teaspoon mill-ground pepper

In a large kettle, sauté onion in 1/4 pound butter or margarine about five minutes. Blend in two tablespoons flour and mix to a paste. Add water slowly and stir until smooth. Add potatoes, celery and carrots and cook vegetables slowly until potatoes are done, about 15 minutes.

In a separate pan, place one or two ounces cooking oil, margarine or butter. Add fish bits and cook over medium heat for 10 to 15 minutes, turning frequently without browning.

Lift fish from oil and add to vegetables. Save oil. Add corn, seasonings and two cups milk to vegetables. Cover, do not boil.

To cooking oil from fish add two tablespoons flour, stirring until smooth. Slowly add two cups milk, continuing to stir until smooth. Add to the kettle. Cover and heat, do not boil.

This recipe by Dr. Jack Field, a Fort Worth pediatrician, was published in *Texas Parks & Wildlife* magazine August 1991

Fishing and Aquatic Programs from Texas Parks and Wildlife

Explore Texas with programs and recreational opportunities from Texas Parks and Wildlife

__ Texas Jr. Angler and Master Angler
    Contact Austin Headquarters at 1-800-792-1112 or 512-389-4755.

__ Project WILD / Aquatic WILD
    Teaching youth (K-12) about using natural resources wisely and sharing the earth with wildlife.
    Texas Parks and Wildlife Education Services 1-800-792-1112 or 512-389-4369.

__ Adopt-A-Wetland
    Teaching youth (K-12) about the ecological importance of wetlands.
    Contact 361-825-3221 or visit on line at www.sci.tamucc.edu/adwp/welcome.htm

__ Texas Freshwater Fisheries Center
    Aquarium and Hatchery Complex near Athens, Texas. View aquatic species in natural settings.
    For tours, contact the TFFC at 903-676-2277.

__ Aquasmart
    School-based safety program shows kids how to be smart when playing in and around water.
    Contact Education services at 512-389-8141 or 512-389-4938.

Visit Texas Parks and Wildlife on line at www.tpwd.state.tx.us

Make A Mini-Minnow Mobile

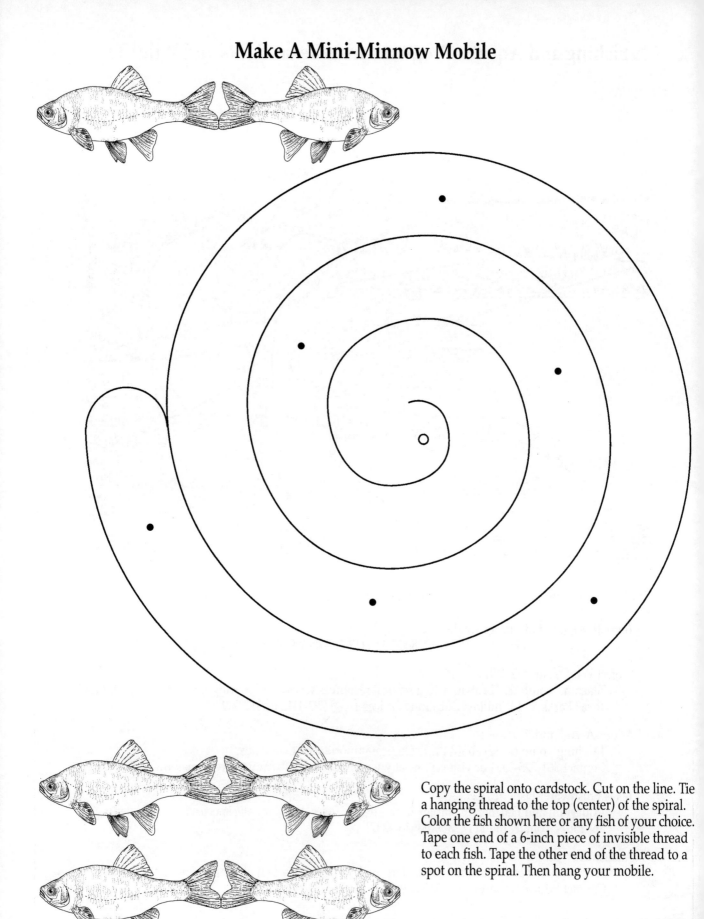

Copy the spiral onto cardstock. Cut on the line. Tie a hanging thread to the top (center) of the spiral. Color the fish shown here or any fish of your choice. Tape one end of a 6-inch piece of invisible thread to each fish. Tape the other end of the thread to a spot on the spiral. Then hang your mobile.

Red Shiner

Make a Fish

Using construction paper, colored paper, scraps of felt etc., copy and cut out the various shapes such as those below or make up your own shapes. Design one or more different fishes for your riverscape. Glue the shapes onto a sheet of paper (you may want to draw an underwater background).

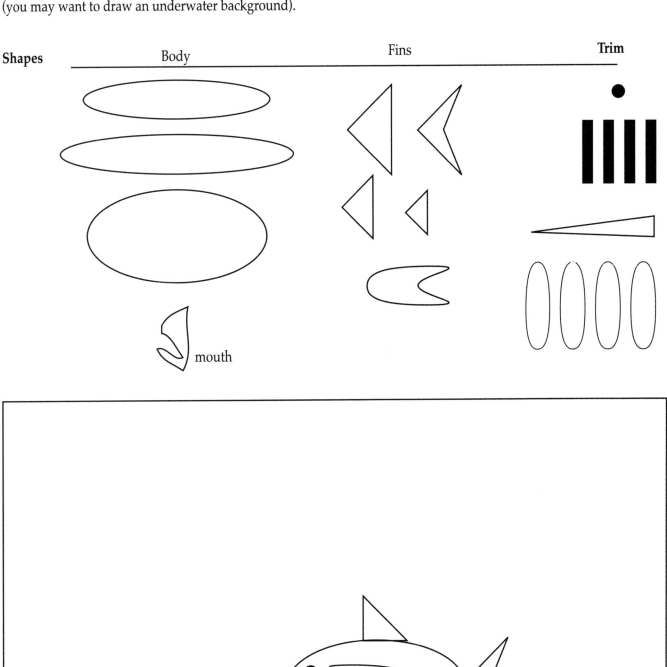

Shapes   Body   Fins   Trim

mouth

Place the Fish in the Fish Bowl

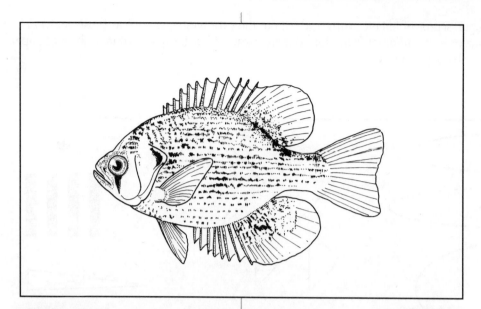

What you'll need:
Cardstock
Colors to decorate your fish
Scissors
Tape or glue
Dowel or long pencil

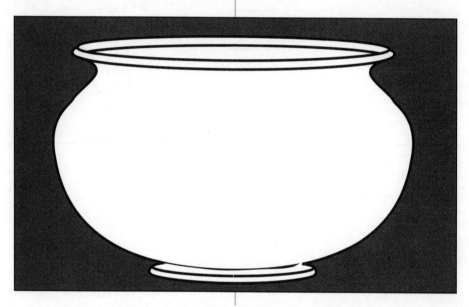

Copy this page onto cardstock.
Color the fish.
Cut out the two rectanglar shapes.
Tape a dowel (or a pencil) along the middle of the back of one of the rectangles (see tick marks for placement).
Tape the two rectangles back to back, (the pencil will be in the middle of the two pieces).
Spin the pencil to see the illusion.

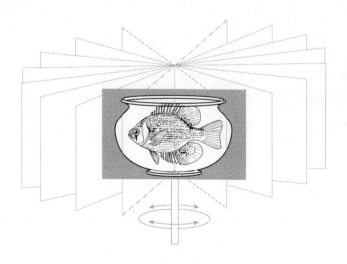

Make a Paper Aquarium for White Bass

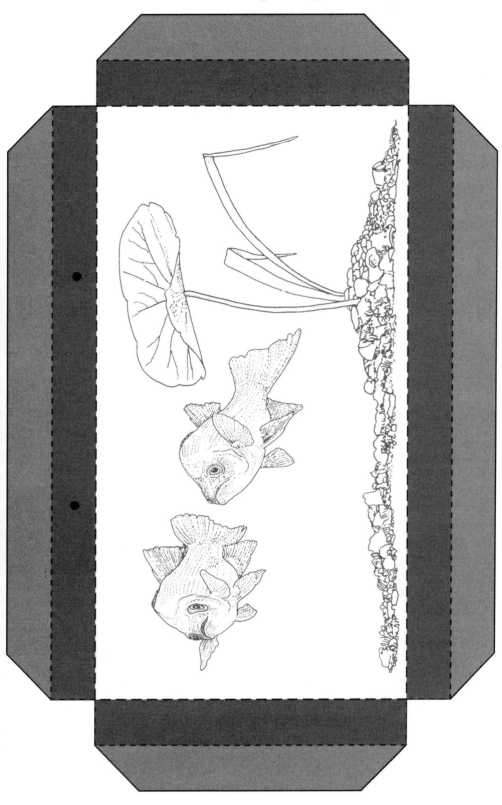

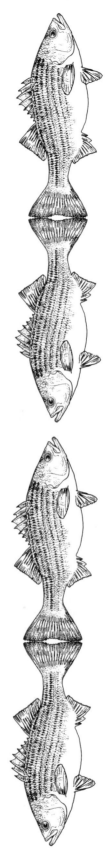

Copy the page onto cardstock. Color the background. Color the fish shown here or make your own. Cut out the shape of the aquarium along the solid lines, fold on the dashed lines. Hang the fish, using tape and thread, to the inside top of the aquarium. Tape the corners together. For a more finished look, tape a 3.5 by 6.5 inch piece of transparent acrylic to the top edge before folding and taping corners.

White Bass

Fish in a Jar

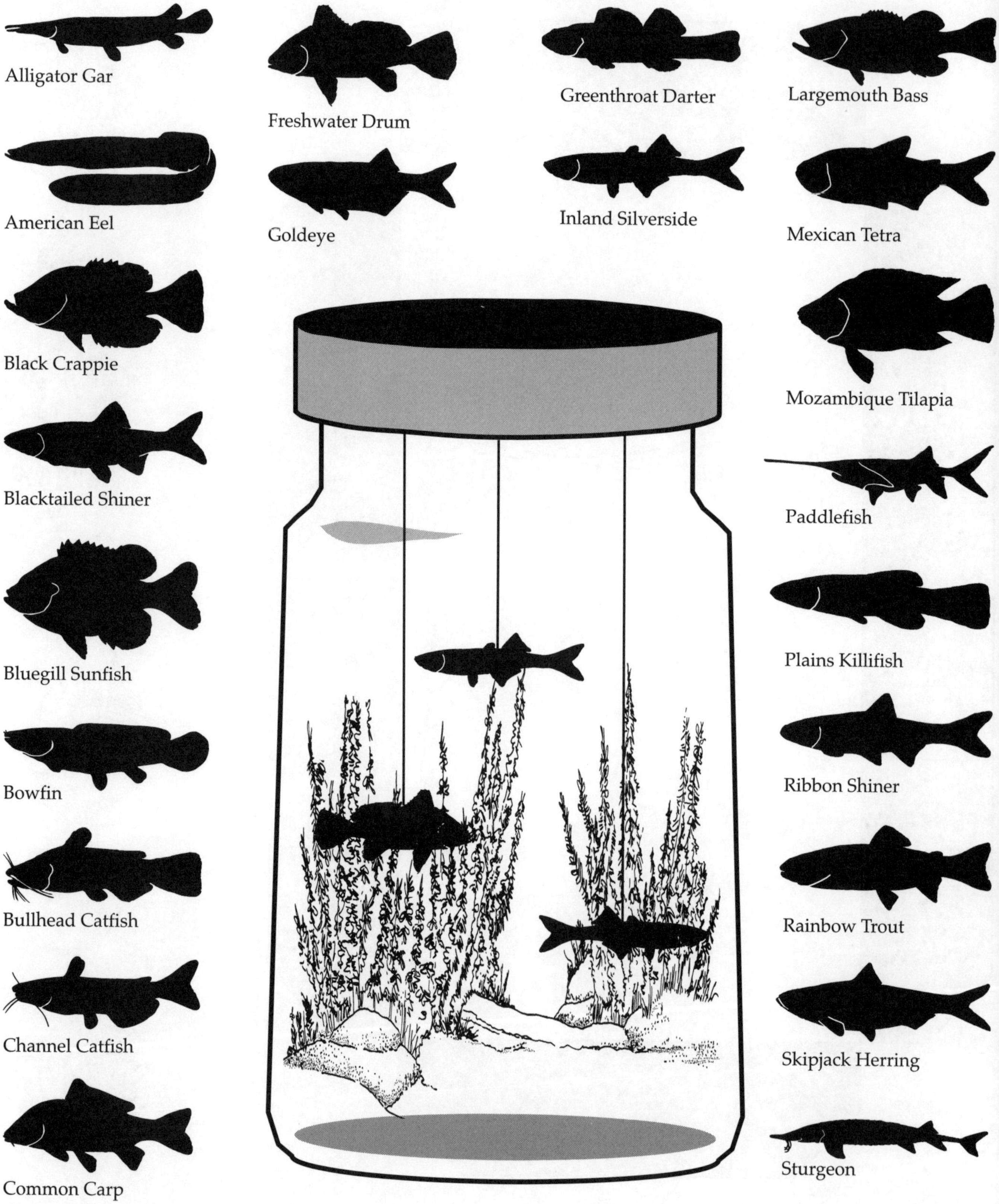

Alligator Gar

American Eel

Black Crappie

Blacktailed Shiner

Bluegill Sunfish

Bowfin

Bullhead Catfish

Channel Catfish

Common Carp

Freshwater Drum

Goldeye

Greenthroat Darter

Inland Silverside

Largemouth Bass

Mexican Tetra

Mozambique Tilapia

Paddlefish

Plains Killifish

Ribbon Shiner

Rainbow Trout

Skipjack Herring

Sturgeon

Use a wide-mouth jar. With acrylic paint, paint an underwater background on the back half of the outside of the jar. To cover the inside bottom of the jar, add sand, small rocks and freshwater shells. Tape one end of a piece of invisible thread to the back of each fish and the other to the lid of the jar. Estimate the length of the thread you need by holding each fish up to the jar. Carefully insert the fish into the jar and tighten the lid.

Fishing Word Puzzle

Find the words in the puzzle. They can be horizontal, vertical or diagonal. Then make a list of the remaining letters and put them together in a sentence. You will have these letters left over: F, I, H, S, R, N, G.

RODS
REELS
FLOATS
FISHING LINE
HOOKS
BAITS
WEIGHTS
SWIVELS
LANDING NET
ANGLER

K	E	E	P	Y	O	U	R	R	O	D	T	S
I	N	F	A	B	A	S	W	I	V	E	L	S
G	A	L	I	N	D	Y	O	U	N	B	R	R
H	O	O	K	S	E	E	L	G	S	A	I	N
A	B	A	O	X	H	B	N	E	T	I	S	W
E	E	T	N	F	I	I	H	S	R	T	N	G
T	R	S	R	O	D	S	N	I	H	S	P	S
A	F	T	E	N	R	F	I	G	S	S	H	I
N	G	C	A	L	E	A	I	N	L	O	F	F
A	N	L	Y	D	I	E	R	T	E	I	O	R
S	A	N	D	F	W	R	O	M	E	Y	N	O
U	R	G	E	A	N	G	L	E	R	A	R	E

___ ___ ___ __ _ ___ ___

___ ____ __ _ __ _____

_____. _____ _____'____ ___

___ ____ __ ___ ___ ___

____.

Hold this page up to a mirror to see the answer.

89

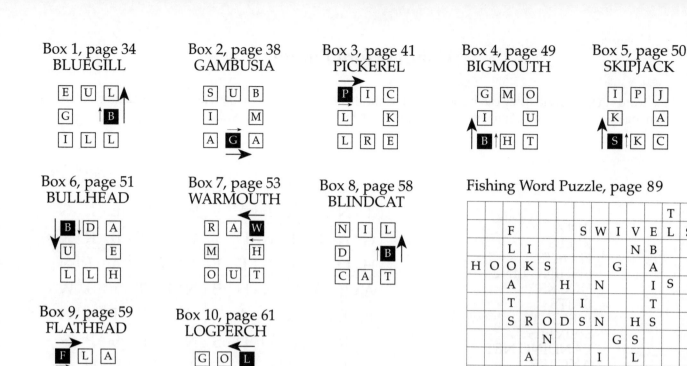

Box 1, page 34
BLUEGILL

E	U	L↑
G	↑B	
I	L	L

Box 2, page 38
GAMBUSIA

S	U	B
I		M
A	G→	A

Box 3, page 41
PICKEREL

P→	I	C
L		K
L	R	E

Box 4, page 49
BIGMOUTH

G	M	O
I		U
↑B	H↑	T

Box 5, page 50
SKIPJACK

I	P	J
↑K		A
↑S	↑K	C

Box 6, page 51
BULLHEAD

B↓	D→	A
U		E
L	L	H

Box 7, page 53
WARMOUTH

R	A	W←
M		H←
O	U	T

Box 8, page 58
BLINDCAT

N	I	L↑
D		↑B↑
C	A	T

Box 9, page 59
FLATHEAD

F→	L	A
D		T
A	E	H

Box 10, page 61
LOGPERCH

G	O	L←
P		H←
E	R	C

Fishing Word Puzzle, page 89

								T		
F			S	W	I	V	E	L	S	
L	I				N	B				
H	O	O	K	S		G		A		
A			H		N		I		S	
T			I			T				
S	R	O	D	S	N		H	S		
	N			G	S					
A			I		L					
L		E		E	I					
	W		E		N					
A	N	G	L	E	R		E			

Fish Seek and Find, page 81

Keep your rods in a bag and your reels in a box between trips. After fishing, clean off any dirt or sand from your gear.

W	E	H	K	C	C	R	E	T	R	A	D	L	G	G	E	H	B
H	K	D	A	L	E	R	E	K	C	I	P	A	A	N	E	S	L
I	I	R	B	H	B	H	R	A	E	D	E	R	M	I	L	I	A
T	P	U	U	L	S	T	R	I	P	E	R	G	B	L	U	F	C
E	F	M	F	I	U	D	A	Y	N	A	A	E	U	N	B	E	K
B	O	W	F	I	N	E	E	G	D	S	I	M	S	S	B	L	B
A	L	N	A	N	F	L	G	I	O	M	N	O	I	S	L	D	A
S	U	A	L	B	N	C	L	I	I	S	B	U	A	A	A	D	S
S	P	O	O	I	O	H	E	R	L	I	O	T	P	B	C	A	S
T	O	O	R	T	C	K	I	R	K	L	W	H	R	E	K	P	H
C	I	B	T	I	B	R	O	C	K	V	T	B	I	P	C	K	E
A	A	L	C	T	J	A	M	A	L	E	R	A	E	U	R	C	E
J	O	T	A	G	E	E	C	G	I	R	O	S	Y	L	A	A	P
R	D	O	F	P	Z	D	M	O	M	S	U	S	E	A	P	J	S
D	A	C	E	I	I	T	B	I	L	I	T	A	L	D	P	P	H
R	E	N	I	H	S	A	O	S	I	D	R	H	L	A	I	I	E
M	O	P	E	R	C	H	O	H	A	E	A	T	A	U	E	K	A
F	L	A	T	H	E	A	D	M	I	N	N	O	W	G	S	D	

Species List of Texas Freshwater Fishes

• Introduced

LAMPREYS

Chestnut Lamprey
Southern Brook Lamprey

STURGEONS

••Shovelnose Sturgeon

PADDLEFISH
Paddlefish

GARS
Alligator Gar
Longnose Gar
••Shortnose Gar
Spotted Gar

BOWFINS
Bowfin

FRESHWATER EELS

American Eel

HERRINGS and SHADS
Gizzard Shad
Shipjack Herring
Threadfin Shad

MOONEYES
••Goldeneye
••Mooneye

TROUTS, SALMONS, CHARS and WHITEFISH
•Rainbow Trout

PIKES
Chain Pickerel
Grass Pickerel
•Northern Pike

CHARACINS
Mexican Tetra

MINNOWS (CYPRINIDS)
•Common Carp
•Grass Carp
•Goldfish
Golden Shiner
••Rio Grande Chub
Creek Chub
Central Stoneroller
Roundnose Minnow
••Devils River Minnow
••Suckermouth Minnow
Longnose Dace
Flathead Chub
Speckled Chub
Mississippi Silvery Minnow
Plains Minnow
••Cypress Minnow
••Striped Shiner
••Redfin Shiner
Ribbon Shiner
••Bluehead Shiner
••Steelcolor Shiner
Blacktail Shiner
••Proserpine Shiner
Edwards Plateau Shiner
Red Shiner
Pugnose Minnow
Flatnose Minnow
••Bluntnose Minnow
Bullhead Minnow
Rio Grande Shiner
Sharpnose Shiner
Emerald Shiner
••Rosyface Shiner

•• Limited Range

Texas Shiner
Silverband Shiner
Chub Shiner
Phantom Shiner
Red River Shiner
Smalleye Shiner
Sabine Shiner
Bigeye Shiner
Weed Shiner
••Ironcolor Shiner
Sand Shiner
Ghost Shiner
Chihuahua Shiner
Mimic Shiner
Tamaulipas Shiner
••Taillight Shiner
Blackspot Shiner
Pallid Shiner

SUCKERS
Smallmouth Buffalo
Bigmouth Buffalo
Black Buffalo
River Carpsucker
Blue Sucker
Spotted Sucker
Creek Chubsucker
Lake Chubsucker
Blacktail Redhorse
Golden Redhorse
Gray Redhorse
West Mexican Redhorse

BULLHEAD CATFISHES
Channel Catfish
Headwater Catfish
Blue Catfish
Yellow Bullhead
Black Bullhead
Flathead Catfish
Widemouth Blindcat
Toothless Blindcat
Tadpole Madtom
Freckled Madtom

SUCKERMOUTH CATFISHES
•Suckermouth Catfish

PIRATE PERCH
Pirate Perch

TOPMINNOWS and KILLIFISHES
Golden Topminnow
Plains Killifish
Blackspotted Topminnow
Western Starhead Topminnow
Blackstrip Topminnow
Rainwater Killifish

PUPFISHES
Pecos Pupfish
Leon Springs Pupfish
Comanche Springs Pupfish
Conchos Pupfish
Red River Pupfish
Sheepshead Minnow

LIVEBEARERS
Sailfin Molly
Amazon Molly
•Guppy
Western Mosquitofish
••Mexican Mosquitofish
Least Killifish
Pecos Gambusia
Clear Creek Gambusia

X Extinct

X San Marcos Gambusia
Big Bend Gambusia
X Amistad Gambusia
X Blotched Gambusia
Largespring Gambusia

SILVERSIDES

Brook Silverside
Inland Silverside
••Rough Silversides (no s?) (Falsom & Amstad Res.)

TEMPERATE BASSES

Striped Bass
White Bass
Yellow Bass

SUNFISHES and BASSES
Banded Pygmy Sunfish
Flier
Black Crappie
White Crappie
Bantam Sunfish
Largemouth bass
Spotted Bass
Guadalupe Bass
Warmouth
Green Sunfish
Spotted Sunfish
Bluegill
Redear Sunfish
Longear Sunfish
Dollar Sunfish
Orangespotted Sunfish
•Redbreasted Sunfish
•Smallmouth Bass
•Rock Bass

DARTERS, PERCHES, WALLEYE and SAUGER

•Walleye
•Sauger
Blackside Darter
Dusky Darter
River Darter
•Yellow Perch
Logperch
Texas Logperch
Bigscale Logperch
Western Sand Darter
Scaly Sand Darter
Bluntnose Darter
Harlequin Darter
Swamp Darter
Mud Darter
Goldstripe Darter
Eastern Redfin Darter
Orangebelly Darter
Greenthroat Darter
Rio Grande Darter
Orangethroat Darter
Cypress Darter
Fountain Darter
Slough Darter

DRUMS
Freshwater Drum

CICHLIDS

Rio Grande Cichlidae
Mozambique Tilapia
Blue Tilapia
Redbelly Tilapia

Use this space to design your own fish.